"*Just Right illustrates the importance and need for a common sense approach to settling legal disputes. It provides the key to settling any legal issue or business disagreement through simplicity and a common sense focus on resolution. Rob Christopher lays out Just the Right approach and blueprint for achieving a fair and economical resolution for both parties.*"

—Frank York, CEO, WL Butler Construction

"*Just Right is a brilliant primer on an innovative approach all can use to deter and resolve common legal disputes at affordable costs in money, time, and peace of mind. Rob Christopher delivers not just a compelling case for better process and outcomes, but practical insights, examples, and resources for how to get both. An insightful must read for all who have felt the bite of over-expensive, unnecessary lawsuits and have yearned for a better solution.*"

—Sharon Reeves, President – Photoflex, Inc.

"*This important book by Rob Christopher hits the proverbial nail on the head. While Just Right is engaging and insightful, its real value is in providing a fair and practical approach to conflict resolution that delivers real justice while saving everyone time and money. Our legal system is slow, cumbersome, and inefficient for most disputes. Just Right is a must read for anyone who seeks to reduce risks for their company. At last, we now have a process that provides business owners a path forward to focus on their business—by quickly resolving disputes outside of a broken system.*"

—Jon W. Ball, Executive Vice President, Hensel Phelps (ret.)

"Finally, it's here!! As a former CEO and after serving over 22 years as a CEO Coach and Silicon Valley Business Advisor, I know that if you stay in business long enough, you will be sued. As a result, this book is the answer we've all been waiting for. . . . *Just Right* is an insightful and innovative approach any leader can use to deter and resolve common legal disputes at an appropriate and equitable level! Rob Christopher delivers not just a compelling case for a better process, but practical advice, clear examples, and specific resources for how to get the job done and the outcome right."

—Lance J. Descourouez, Master Chair with Vistage International

"The NDR process described in Just Right *has saved me thousands of dollars and much time resolving disputes that were headed toward legal action. By using the NDR process, we spent our time focused on growing our business, not battling frivolous, frustrating and costly lawsuits. If you have faced disputes or frustrating lengthy legal battles, this book is a must read.*"

—Bryan Hoadley, CEO Podium Advisors

"During my forty years as a lawyer, I've experienced first-hand the impact of a legal system that's structured to work for the big and wealthy, but not for the average person with a simple dispute. Change is necessary, and Just Right *provides an important step in that direction. Insightful, clear, and innovative, the solutions offered in* Just Right *are what attorneys and individuals need to move beyond the current sclerotic system. It should be mandatory reading for everyone in the legal system and for anyone who may be faced with a dispute or legal situation.*"

—Robert Sloss, Partner, Procopio

Just Right

How Neutral-Driven
Resolution Can Close the Gap
in American Civil Justice

Robert Christopher

Published by FAIR MISSION PRESS
Copyright © 2022 by Robert Christopher
All rights reserved.

This publication is designed to provide accurate and authoritative information in regard
to the subject matter covered. It is sold with the understanding that neither the author
nor the publisher is hereby engaged in offering or rendering legal or other professional
services. If legal advice or other expert assistance is required, the services of a competent professional should be retained.

LIBRARY OF CONGRESS CATALOGING-IN-PUBLICATION DATA
Names: Christopher, Robert (Robert A.), 1953- author.
Title: Just right : how neutral-driven resolution can close the gap in American civil
justice / Robert Christopher.
Description: Morgan Hill, CA : Fair Mission Press, [2022]
Identifiers: ISBN: 979-8-9853949-0-0 (paperback) | 979-8-9853949-1-7 (ebook) |
979-8-9853949-2-4 (audio-stores) | 979-8-9853949-3-1 (audio-libraries)
Subjects: CSH: Dispute resolution (Law)—United States. | Mediation—United States. |
Arbitration agreements, Commercial—United States. | Compromise (Law)—United
States. | Arbitration and award—United States. | Conflict management--United States. |
Justice, Administration of—United States. | BISAC: BUSINESS & ECONOMICS /
Conflict Resolution & Mediation.
Classification: LCC: KF9084 .C57 2022 | DDC: 347.73/9—dc23

To Dad, who taught me the value of work.
To Mom, who encouraged me to dream.
To Ginny and the kids, who deliver the joy
and bear my distractions.

TABLE OF CONTENTS

FOREWORD

"The power of hope upon human exertion and happiness is wonderful."

—Abraham Lincoln

Abraham Lincoln, one of America's preeminent statesmen and lawyers, would appreciate Rob Christopher's new book, *Just Right*—in large part because Christopher's work brings bright beams of hope and light to the traditional judicial process. Luminaries such as Washington, Franklin, and Douglass sought to rally their audiences to make bold steps forward, to break the chains of outdated thinking, to steward us into the New World, to see things differently. The spirit of this courage resides in all of us, but true innovators are a rare species. How many of us would still be satisfied to read by a candle, but for Edison's blessing us with the incandescent light? After reading Christopher's book, decide for yourself whether there is now room for such enlightenment in the gnarled branches of conflict resolution.

Like many, I've had the opportunity to experience both mediation and the court system. If I told you that I sold the former clubhouse of a California golf course and the buyer sought legal recourse because I didn't disclose the course was noisily mowed early in the morning, you might accuse me of an unbridled imagination and check to see if I was wearing a tin-foil hat. There's more to the actual story, including a "compromise" demand that I pay for triple-pane windows. Truth may be stranger than fiction—but know that four attorneys and a retired judge were all well-compensated to resolve that bald-faced assault on my sanity.

So, when Christopher, an experienced litigator, came to me with a plan on how frivolous disputes of modest size could be deterred and unavoidable ones could be settled fairly and inexpensively in weeks rather than years, he found a willing audience.

In this timely book, Christopher brings a can-do spirit of practicality and forward-thinking to calcified, archaic, and often unfair legal process. *Just Right* explains in well-organized, succinct chapters how tough disputes can be resolved in a just *and* efficient manner. From my perspective as a businessperson, I find it especially refreshing to have a process that truly saves business owners, vendors, customers, and employees serious time and money when disputes rear their ugly heads. This kind of process might even save a few relationships.

The approach, called Neutral-Driven Resolution or "NDR," invites everyone involved in the lifeblood of commerce and other relationships to agree—either *before* trouble arises or, if necessary, *when* it does—to a better, more dignified way to solve legal differences that defy amicable settlement. The easy-to-follow, non-adversarial technique he evangelizes provides clear benefits to all concerned—except those lawyers who demand too big a piece of a small pie. For those legal professionals interested in prioritizing their time and championing their clients' welfare, *Just Right* serves as an excellent primer.

Conflict drives the plotlines of the world's greatest literature, whether your tastes range from Twain to Tolstoy, offering teachable moments for all of us. But when one's own money and time are at stake, it's not the stuff of fiction. In *Just Right*, Christopher heralds a coming, real-world revolution, bolstered by his extensive experience as a skilled litigator. We hear a veteran's wisdom, rather than a theorist's ivory tower imaginings, as Christopher emerges from his distinguished career with a crucial epiphany: *"Limited stakes" disputes deserve better than to be resolved in courtroom fights between notoriously expensive legal teams.* Granted, traditional mediation and arbitration stand as well-intended attempts at sidestepping the legal morass, but Christopher pulls the wheels off these older wagons and places them onto a modern NDR supercar which allows *all* contestants to finish faster, cheaper, and with greater dignity.

The choice of book title isn't by happenstance, and we, as readers, should take note. The title acknowledges from the very beginning that a "one-size-fits-all" approach doesn't work for legal disagreements any more than it does for shoes and hats. Christopher unambiguously explains that limited stakes, like beauty and art, are in the eye of the beholder—the author's genius is giving both sides of the negotiating table the *flexibility* to decide, based on their circumstances, what kinds and sizes of disputes are so limited and what process will be *just right* to resolve them. Moreover, Christopher also explains that the neutral-driven approach to solving potential differences complements, rather than replaces, the adversarial approach to justice: For issues where the constituents' stakes are large, traditional avenues to redress still have their place.

If you've ever had a golf or tennis lesson, you know how discrete improvements can help you straighten your drive or lower unforced errors. I found similar gems in every chapter of this fine book, so I recommend a full read. And Christopher has worked hard to make the topic approachable with a conversational writing style and welcome elements of humor and humility. Like all great teachers, he explains the complex with efficacy. Nevertheless, those readers with limited time for a topic that hopefully won't arise often in their lives can cut to the proverbial chase by reading the summaries at the end of each chapter.

This reader's takeaway? *Just Right* is a must read for both those in the legal profession and ordinary folks who seek speedy and fair resolutions to time-killing and unnecessarily expensive disputes.

If I were to paraphrase Christopher's neutral-driven approach, it's essentially a way "to cut through the bull durham." And, as someone who grew up on a cattle ranch, I'm all for that.

Peter Coe Verbica,
Managing Director, Silicon Private Wealth
Author, *Hard-Won Cowboy Wisdom*

PREFACE

WHY I WROTE THIS BOOK

I am both a businessman and a career lawyer. And yes, that may make me a living oxymoron.

As a businessman, I see that lawyers cost too much, lawsuits waste and distract precious time, and consequently, legal justice often costs far more than it's worth. I rebel at this gross inefficiency and the loss of hard-earned profit that most Americans know (or strongly suspect) seriously undermine the overall cause of justice in our society. Meanwhile, the lawyer in me sees this travesty and is chagrined by my profession's ineffective problem-solving here in failing to serve the best interests of our clients and the ideal of justice.

The greater tragedy, however, is that these outcomes are largely avoidable. After three decades of dutiful professional service accompanied by growing awareness, frustration, and insight, I came to the conclusion that I really had no choice: I had to do something about it. If no one else was going to champion a real solution to this problem, I would.

Now, I didn't write this book to bash lawyers, even though I conclude that we rely on lawyers for their advocacy in many more legal disputes than we should. Instead, I wrote this with my business and client hats on, in other words from the perspective of consumers of legal services, to do two things. First, I cast a bright light on a huge and growing problem in resolving common legal disputes in America. Second, I offer a simple and practical tool we can all adopt in our businesses and in our personal lives that will improve our net outcomes, financial bottom lines, the usefulness of our time, and our peace of mind. Not coincidentally, win or lose, these better outcomes also create more real justice that respects both economic proportion and personal dignity.

The oxymoron label may be especially apt for yet another reason. This book violates a recommended practice in book-writing to choose a single ideal reader profile, and then align the book's writing style, language, and message with that person's likely tastes and perspectives. For several reasons, it has been necessary to write this book for two very different audiences: First and foremost are businesspeople and other consumers (i.e., clients) of legal services, most of whom lack legal training. Second—but equally critical because of their gatekeeper and expert professional roles in the American legal system—are lawyers and others trained in the law.

The kind of innovation championed in this book requires the buy-in, or at least open-mindedness of lawyers and clients alike. The writing challenge is that lawyers are trained to read, write, and process ideas in legal terms, while their clients are not. Consequently, I've done my best to address both audiences, trying to write less like a lawyer and being aware to define and explain necessary legal terms wherever possible. I've even made a point to throw almost all footnotes—much beloved by lawyers—to the end of the book, and to close every chapter with a one-page summary that each reader—lawyer and nonlawyer alike—can reference whenever you find your attention waning or you'd just like a quick review.

What I passionately want is for each of you to develop real understanding about the growing gap in American civil justice addressed here, empowering knowledge of what you can do about it, and the confidence (or at least curiosity) to take a simple step or two that will return better, faster, and more affordable justice.

"The men are excited about getting to shoot a lawyer."

CHAPTER 1

INTRODUCTION: NO WAY TO WIN

"War is the unfolding of miscalculation."
—Barbara Tuckman

There was no way to win. We just didn't know it yet.

My client was a small animal testing laboratory owned by a husband and wife team. He was the business manager; she the scientist. Except for their advanced degrees, they resembled every other pair of devoted partners I knew. Sure, they would bicker, they could be stubborn and myopic, but they were ethical, well-intentioned people who believed in doing the right thing.

As decent people, they didn't like the idea of harming animals—even rodents—unnecessarily. They did, however, see the need to apply learning and skills humanely so that scientific medical advances with genuine potential for saving lives and reducing suffering could be brought to the market. I liked them, and they seemed to like me—as much as anyone can really "like" their lawyer while paying for help that should not have been necessary. In any event, they also trusted me, as I had effectively helped them through legal scrapes before, and, wherever I could, I advocated for solutions that made sense for them economically as well as legally.

This particular dispute started, as many do, with an outstanding bill. A start-up pharmaceutical company had contracted with the lab to test the efficacy of an experimental cancer treatment on custom bred mice. Unfortunately, the test results weren't favorable, which jeopardized both the start-up's potential FDA certification and a future round of venture capital financing. Desperate for positive results, and unwilling to disclose its potential predicament, the start-up blamed the lab. It claimed without explanation that the lab must have performed the study incompetently, refused to pay the balance due for the testing done to date, and demanded a redo of the study at no cost.

For the lab, at stake was about $47,000 owed, plus the value to the start-up of the remaining mice. While the case wasn't a "bet-the-company" or precedent-setting dispute that merited a whatever it takes approach, that $47,000 was the *entire* profit the lab stood to make on the project. For the start-up, a favorable outcome to the dispute would enable more testing at no additional cost, likely earning it precious time to attract new capital.

Both sides quickly realized that possession of the mice was the key leverage to favorably resolving the dispute, as the mice were both the lab's collateral for the balance due on the study and a practical necessity for any additional testing. The situation was made especially time-sensitive because these mice were required to be bred with autoimmune deficiencies, and the sad fact was that their life spans were shorter than normal mice. In these circumstances, with each side appearing to want something the other had, I initially felt reaching an early settlement was realistic and achievable via either direct negotiation or mediation.

BRIEF

Appendix A is a glossary of most legal terms used in this book.

DARTH LAWYER STRIKES BACK

But there was a problem. The start-up's CEO was the kind of person who thinks he's the smartest in any room and seeks to intimidate all around him. He was also an attorney. In my experience, attorneys with this unique blend of ego, myopia, and self-interest are driven to push aggressive courses of action that go well beyond the point where it should be obvious things aren't going as planned.

In hindsight, I'm pretty sure that's what happened here. Since I wasn't privy to the conversations among this lawyer CEO, his board, and investors, I can't say for sure what he told them, but I've seen this happen often enough in my career that I'm confident in my assessment. Not surprisingly, this CEO also appeared to believe he could save the start-up money by legally representing his own company and forcing an early, one-sided outcome in his favor. What's that adage about the lawyer who represents himself having a fool for a client?

After the first round of letters, calls, and unreasonable demands from the other side, I warned my client that unless we could get a neutral mediator to help the parties settle early, the lab's legal fees in this case likely would exceed the $47,000 at stake. Thinking, quite logically, that its possession of the mice would force the other side to see reason, the lab was unwilling to surrender its rights. The husband and wife partners were tired of taking losses on valid studies when clients didn't get the desired results (an occupational hazard in their business). They were prepared, therefore, to take a principled stand either in mediation or, if that failed, court. Soon enough, their hands were forced, as the other side dismissed my suggestion of early mediation and moved in federal district court for a preliminary injunction (a type of court order) to turn over the mice to the start-up.

Now, good litigators know that these kinds of injunctions—to change, rather than just preserve, the status quo—are uphill battles with judges, especially early in a case that is at best a "he-said/she-said" toss-up where the party seeking the injunction may well have failed to behave fairly toward the other. Unfortunately, my adversary was already invested in his strategy and didn't want to listen to reason. In any event, $12,000 in legal fees later, the judge denied the injunction and my client kept possession of the mice. We took a breath and hoped for a new attitude, or at least some rationality—even if it were hidden behind the usual bluster of overconfident rhetoric from the other side. Unfortunately, the start-up's lawyer CEO doubled down on aggression. The fight had just begun.

Before I continue, let me address the question nonlawyers may be asking right about now: How is it possible to spend $12,000 in legal fees to defeat a single motion in a modest case? I could break this down by hourly rate, filing fees, and court expenses, but that would deliver merely an unhelpful tally of dollars. The reality is that the smallest case, once accepted, can be just as challenging, just as complicated, and just as hard-fought as the largest. Consequently, the tasks of competently gathering, organizing, and presenting evidence, and researching and making legal arguments, seldom correlate with the amount of money at stake. Moreover, every attorney advocate is hard-wired to fight for their client and spurred on by training, the ethical duty of zealous representation, and the ever-present shadow of possible liability for malpractice.

WEAPONS OF MASS DESTRUCTION

Next came the discovery wars. Discovery is the formal pre-trial process in lawsuits by which parties request and obtain evidence and other relevant information from each other. Methods of discovery include depositions (recorded oral testimony), exchanges of records and things, written interrogatories (questions), and requests to stipulate that certain facts are undisputed. As a practical matter, discovery is *always* partially insane. The combination of need, procedural weapons and rules, strategies to burden or retaliate, and competing egos all inevitably inflate the process and its costs—even among attorneys with the best of intentions. This case was no exception.

If you've had to endure lawsuit discovery even once, then you already know what too often happens: Legal costs quickly get out of control. Perhaps the best way to communicate the incredible waste that occurs is to track the path of just one simple, common question and answer among dozens in a case like this.

> *As a practical matter, discovery is always partially insane. The combination of need, procedural weapons and rules, strategies to burden or retaliate, and competing egos all inevitably inflate the process and its costs—even among attorneys with the best of intentions.*

Conventional wisdom has it that written interrogatories to identify witnesses and other key facts are a good way to cut to the chase and save money. There are other opening moves, but each has drawbacks and similar opportunities for maneuver and delay. In the lab case, we began by asking the other side to identify, in writing, who worked on the project on their side and what they did, as this would help us streamline the depositions we'd need to take. We needed a complete answer that we could rely on (in other words, the equivalent of sworn testimony by the company), so we couldn't just ask over the phone and trust verbal answers. Consequently, we carefully crafted an interrogatory (one of several), including the usual precisely worded instructions and definitions in order to minimize the risk of genuine confusion and to prevent any legitimate objections. Once again, the clock on legal fees started to tick.

Thirty days later, when the response was due, opposing counsel asked for more time to gather the information. In litigation, it *never* pays to refuse the other side's first request to extend a time deadline—it's part courtesy, part golden rule, and part good appearances if a visit to court proves necessary. We gave him two weeks. Tick.

Opposing counsel immediately sent over his own counter set of interrogatories. Tick.

Two weeks later, he sent his formal response, which consisted purely of objections. Tick.

Procedural rules don't permit attorneys simply to call "Bullshit" by immediately bringing in court a motion to compel the information. First, we had to send a "meet-and-confer" letter, outlining the shortcomings in the response to date and asking for a prompt meeting to confer about them. Tick.

The opposing counsel asked for more time. Tick.

We followed up by telephone and email. Tick.

A date was set. Tick.

We prepared for the meeting. Tick.

The afternoon before the meeting, opposing counsel's office called to postpone because of an "unexpected" schedule conflict. Tick.

The parties renegotiated a new date two weeks later. Tick.

We prepared for the meeting a second time. Tick.

The meet-and-confer finally took place, resolving little, because the other guy's agenda was to simply burden the lab with more legal costs having nothing to do with giving or getting truth. Tick.

We researched and prepared a motion to compel the requested information. Tick.

In order to get a hearing date, we had to coordinate with opposing counsel. Tick.

Opposing counsel read our motion and then researched, prepared, and filed an opposition. We read his opposition, then researched and submitted a short brief in response. Tick, tick.

The day before the scheduled hearing on the motion, the court issued a tentative ruling granting our motion and ordering the start-up to pay "sanctions" covering some of my legal fees, the latter because the opposition did not have a substantial justification for failing to answer our question in the first place. The start-up CEO, as opposing counsel, advised the court that he planned to appear and argue the motion orally, so we duly notified the court that we would be there too. Tick.

Knowing courts favor those who present succinct arguments, both sides prepared by outlining key points they wanted to make efficiently, and by anticipating questions the court might ask and any oral arguments from opposing counsel. Tick.

At the hearing, opposing counsel seemed more interested in nullifying the sanctions order through a litany of excuses than arguing against our motion. The court, not wishing to start the case appearing unduly critical of counsel from another jurisdiction (more courtesy), gave him the benefit of some imagined doubt and retracted the order for sanctions. Afterward, I had to explain to my clients why they were forced to bear the additional costs of yet another fight they'd won. Tick, tick.

Two weeks later, we got a one-page answer bearing six names and cryptic descriptions of each witness' role in the project. The answers were so deficient that we could have brought another motion requesting clarification. Of course, we didn't. What is that definition of insanity?

We went through similar battles over *records* discovery, which also resounded with the same tick, tick, tick of the legal fees clock.

After a few months of this kind of costly discovery nonsense, my clients, to their credit, realized this had to stop. We'd already spent more than half of the $47,000 that they stood to win, while depositions, trial preparation, pre-trial motions, and trial still lay ahead. The painfully obvious truth was there was no way they could be made whole financially.

Fortunately for us, time was running down on the life span of the special mice. Also, the start-up's board of directors appeared to be getting frustrated and testy with their CEO lawyer. The parties finally agreed to mediate, as the lab and I had suggested six months and about $25,000 ago.

We picked a mediator. Tick.

We coordinated a date. Tick.

We wrote mediation briefs with extensive attached exhibits. Tick, tick.

We all met with the mediator for a day and cut a deal that no one liked. Tick, tick.

We documented it as a stipulated judgment for over $40,000. Tick.

We delivered the mice in return for a large down payment, about $10,000, on the agreed settlement amount, suspecting that we might never get the rest. Tick.

The start-up contracted with another lab for its remaining trials, and when those too failed, the company went bankrupt before making any more settlement payments. My clients wanted me to try to enforce the judgment, possibly against an arguable successor corporation. That would earn me more money, but almost certainly not make them whole. I talked them out of it. One last tick.

I had done excellent legal work. I had given sound advice in my clients' best interests and won when forced to fight. *Yet they were worse off, and I felt I had failed them.* **Figure 1** is a summary of their financial equation in this case at the time they settled.

FIGURE 1 My Clients' Financial Equation at the Time of Mediation.

Item	Actual (as settled)	Projected (through trial)
Stakes/Max. Recovery	$40,000	$47,000
Legal Costs	-$35,000	-$75,000
Lost Work Time	-$8,000	-$18,000
Net Recovery or Loss	-$3,000*	-$51,000
Duration	9 months	>1.5 years

* Clients' Net Loss later increased by $30,000 when the start-up dissolved after paying only $10,000 of the settlement

More accurately, our justice system had failed them. I was struck for the umpteenth time by an overwhelmingly clear fact: ***Only a miniscule portion of the profuse hours and money that each side put into the case—and virtually none of the time and energy distracted from other work—had anything to do with answering the core question in dispute.***

The whole process was largely waste, loss, futility, and wholly unwarranted when compared with what was at stake.

A NO-MAN'S-LAND OF INJUSTICE: THE LIMITED STAKES DILEMMA

For thirty-seven years, I litigated mostly business cases. I served as advocate, consultant, client, arbitrator, mediator, and settlement judge. I was blessed to have a farm upbringing that led me to appreciate hard work and the dollars paid for it, an enviable formal education, and a top peer and judiciary rating of legal ability and professional ethics.

I've worked on hundreds of cases, and shared stories with count-less lawyers, companies, and individuals. That broad experience has taught me two powerful truths about my profession and our adver-sarial legal system:

- In **high stakes** situations, lawyers are both necessary and worth all the trouble, distraction, and expense, because in those cases, we generally increase the quality and quantity of justice in our society.

- However, in what I will call **limited stakes** situations—and these constitute the vast majority of disputes that arise in business and life—unless we negotiate an almost immediate settlement, *dueling lawyers aren't worth it, don't make sense, and can't make sense,* because the multiple costs of attorney advocacy and formal legal process inevitably approach or exceed what is at stake.

Let's take this moment to define these terms so we're all on the same page: Stakes are *high* when it makes sense to spend whatever time, money, and peace of mind are needed either to win (subjective) or get it right (objective). For example, a capital murder case is plain-ly high stakes. A human life hangs in the balance. The same is true for many criminal offenses in which years of freedom or life-defining reputations are at stake. On the civil (i.e., noncriminal) side, a child custody or "bet-the-company" dispute, and *any* dispute involving mil-lions of dollars of loss, all probably qualify as **high stakes**. Similarly, a powerful argument can be made that the stakes are high in any dispute that will set a precedent affecting basic human or constitutional rights.

At the other end of the spectrum are **small claims** disputes, which each state defines by law based on the dollar amount in dispute. In most states today, small claims top out in the range of $5,000 to $10,000. Special small claims courts administer these disputes, which typically *prohibit* representation by legal counsel and conduct expe-dited judge-trials similar to (but usually much less entertaining than) those seen on popular television shows like *Judge Judy.*

Between the two are **limited stakes** disputes, characterized by one overriding reality: *Win or lose, most or all of the money or equivalent value at stake is likely to be consumed by legal fees and related costs through the course of any adversarial legal process such as trial, arbitration, or even mediation.*

In other words, these are disputes for which our adversarial system *cannot* deliver real and economically rational justice. Most responsible, client-centric lawyers dislike these cases and avoid them whenever possible, because they know that if they can't settle early, they won't be able to deliver a satisfactory net outcome to their clients beyond the possibility of vindication or bragging rights. In practice, many of these lawyers believe the limited stakes range falls between the upper small claims limit and about $300,000 to $500,000.

> *Limited stakes disputes are characterized by one overriding reality: Win or lose, most or all of the money or equivalent value at stake is likely to be consumed by legal fees and related costs through the course of any adversarial legal process such as trial, arbitration, or even mediation.*

There's another, corollary reality that I need mention. I state it separately here, in part because this is a piece of the limited stakes dilemma that most attorneys don't see or are loathe to admit, and in part because it's true irrespective of the absurd costs of getting real justice in this no-man's-land: *In limited stakes disputes, except in the rare situation where there is not a competent lawyer on the other side, the advocacy of lawyers in any formal legal process will not make a sufficient difference in the outcome to pay for itself.*

In other words, if each of the attorneys involved is at least minimally competent, then the combination of limited stakes, the controlling influences of the facts and governing law in the hands of a neutral judge, and the unpredictable vagaries of chance will generally overwhelm whatever influence superior advocacy could have. Only mistaken self-importance or self-interest leads us to think otherwise. For the client in a limited stakes dispute, therefore, retaining legal services beyond initial assessment, negotiation, and sometimes ongoing advice makes no economic sense whatsoever. **Figure 2** illustrates this corollary reality.

FIGURE 2 What Wins a Dispute?

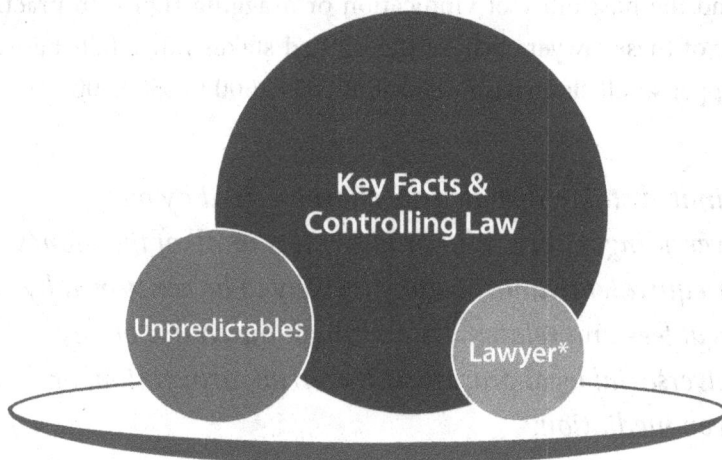

* Assumes that each side has at least competent counsel

Unfortunately, there is little explicit data on this topic because such information is detrimental to the interests of the legal profession, seldom tracked, and largely confidential. It's true nonetheless, based on what evidence *is* available (to be presented later) and on the kind of probability analysis that any mathematician worth his or her salt could readily demonstrate. I also know it to be true because I and countless others have witnessed and lived it repeatedly. Many times during my career I outclassed or thought I had outclassed an adversary, or saw another attorney plainly outclass an adversary, only to see the outcome go contrary to those perceptions, because of factors—usually the facts or law—outside the better advocate's ability to overcome.

DETHRONING PRETENDERS

If the limited stakes problem is that obvious, there ought to be a solution. In the United States, well-meaning people have looked for an answer since the early twentieth century. An entire industry, appropriately labeled **Alternative Dispute Resolution (ADR)**, was spawned in large part to address this. New methods of resolving disputes have taken hold despite initial resistance from much of the bar. For example, both arbitration and mediation (discussed in Chapter 3) are now embraced by many lawyers as faster and cheaper alternatives to going to court. This love affair, however, seems to correlate directly with the extent to which these methods have been "lawyerized" or, as some critics would say, "corrupted" by a self-interested legal profession that supplies too many of our legislators and all of our judges.

BRIEF

"Bar" is legalese for licensed attorneys. The term's origin stems from the use of physical bars of wood that separated the observing public from the working spaces in early courtrooms.

More fairly, I believe the shortcomings in these alternatives lie mostly in myopic zeal, good intentions, and insidious procedural creep, which are even more difficult to overcome than acknowledged evils like avarice and ignorance. Attorneys believe in the power of lawyer-driven process to deliver justice, so we keep complicating new methods originally intended to simplify and expedite resolutions, thereby assuring greater need for our advocacy. Regardless of the cause, these alternatives unfortunately have become *mini-me's* of lit-igation that still suffer from the inability to deliver real and economic justice in most limited stakes situations.

WHAT IF...

It makes sense then, that a real solution, if there is one, must lie outside the box of traditional lawyer-driven process. A real solution must be able to deliver judicial-quality outcomes at a cost that consumes only a reasonable fraction of the value at stake—both in time and money. Simple, practical, and easy to adopt, a real solution should respect *everyone's* time, energy, dignity, and peace of mind, allowing us to be better partners and neighbors. It should protect us against both the thieves among us and our own mistakes and darker selves, without forcing us to compromise our principles. The real solution should be a tool that allows lawyers to operate in ways that truly help their clients, while discouraging or even disabling behaviors that don't. In short, any real solution must *truly* increase the quantity and quality of real justice in our society. At this point, doubt that such a solution exists would be understandable. Sadly, our much beloved legal system and lawyers' egos have brainwashed us not to see the possibility and po-tential for a real solution, not to believe in it, and not to use it when we should, so it's going to take a wake-up call for lawyers and nonlawyers alike to make it happen. The very good news is that a solution does exist. Hence this book.

CHAPTER SUMMARY

- An ordinary commercial dispute between a testing laboratory and a cancer drug start-up company over a sum of $47,000 illustrates the typical course, wasted time, and economic insanity of such lawsuits today.

- This case and consistent experience over a 40-year career reveal two powerful truths about lawsuits:

  — In **high stakes** situations, battling lawyers generally are both necessary and worth what they cost, because their efforts increase the quality and quantity of justice enjoyed by the parties and our society. Examples of high stakes are murder and other serious crimes, "bet-the-company" and multimillion-dollar civil lawsuits, and cases resolving important human or constitutional rights.

  — In **limited stakes** situations, however, unless the parties or their lawyers negotiate a settlement almost immediately (or the dispute belongs in small claims court where lawyers are excluded), the many costs of lawyers' advocacy through a formal legal process like court will consume most or all of the money value at stake. This effectively prevents real, economically rational justice. Unfortunately, the vast majority of legal disputes that arise in business and life fall into this category of limited stakes ranging from about $10,000 to $500,000 or more.

- A corollary truth is that, where stakes are limited, unless one side's lawyer is wholly incompetent (a rare event), superior lawyering in either court or similar legal process is highly unlikely to make enough difference in outcome to pay for itself. The combination of limited stakes, the controlling influences of the actual facts and governing law in the hands of a neutral judge, and unpredictable vagaries of chance will generally overwhelm and render uneconomic any gains from having the "better" lawyer.

- An entire industry, called **ADR** (for **Alternative Dispute Resolution**), has emerged to counter this problem. ADR includes lawyer-led resolution methods like arbitration and mediation. Unfortunately, these methods increasingly have become *mini-me's* of adversarial litigation that still fail to deliver justice at reasonable cost in most limited stakes situations.

- A real solution, if there is one, must lie outside the box of traditional lawyer-driven process. In America, lawyers and clients alike have been brainwashed to believe no such solution exists. That belief is mistaken.

"And for God's sake stay as far away as you can from the legal system—unless, of course you're a lawyer."

CHAPTER 2

MY STORY: I ARE ONE

Before we go any further together, you're entitled to know more about me. Not because my life to date is book-worthy. I don't think it is. You're entitled to know whether my upbringing, experience, values, and likely motivations make me worthy of your trust. To that end, let me begin as comedian Jeff Foxworthy often does when joking about rednecks, by admitting that "I are one" of the lawyers whom I address in this book.

This book champions real innovation—controversial to some—that rejects traditional norms and swims against the current of how we Americans usually process common legal disputes. Most lawyers will nod their heads and say that the tool I describe in this book is welcome and long overdue. Many, however, will then engage in passive-aggressive resistance by never seriously considering, learning about, recommending, or using it—knowing full well that they are their clients' gatekeepers to all things legal. Whether this is done out of self-interest, ignorance, or both, makes little difference, as the result is the same. Therefore, if I am going to convince *you* to invite and use—when it makes sense—a very different solution to legal disputes, there needs to be trust between us. On the other hand, if you're willing to reject or accept my premises and conclusions on their logical merit alone, feel free to skip ahead to the Chapter Summary.

MY FIRST TIME

No one forgets their first time. I certainly won't. As you would expect, it had four phases: raw desire, fear of disappointing, the big thrill, and ultimately real learning.

I speak of my first trial. The year was 1981. I was a second-year associate at a venerable downtown Los Angeles law firm. The trial was in Orange County. After waiting two years for the opportunity, I was thrilled. I was also scared. I feared that I faced an uphill battle representing an unsympathetic big business, and that my inexperience might cost my client dearly. On the very first day, I did the unthinkable: I stepped from my counsel table into the well—the area in front of the judge's bench and witness stand—without asking permission. The bailiff jumped out of his chair. I turned around, momentarily stupefied. The judge waived him off and gently explained. I apologized and confessed my rookie status, the latter unnecessary in hindsight. Not a great start, and a bit unnerving.

Fortunately, as the trial progressed, I found I had the three things needed to help me win: a forgiving senior judge who didn't mind mentoring a first-timer in the nuances of real (not TV) courtroom etiquette, a solid and likeable old-school witness whom I could promote as the human face of my client, and, most importantly, a truthful story that I could tell with credible passion. So I became a dutiful student again, let my witness be himself, and delivered a compelling closing argument (by my opponents' post-trial assessments). The euphoric thrill I experienced when judgment came was like those rare moments in younger days when I was blessed to win a "big game" with a last-second score. This thrill, however, lasted longer and meant more, because I felt like a hero who had made a difference for the good of someone else, and it confirmed to me that I had chosen the right profession. The client, who was used to losing similar cases, was most happy, and my stock at the law firm climbed several notches.

I tell this story not to brag—I've certainly lost trials since—but rather to set the table for sharing with you the completely unexpected personal frustration and learning I experienced following that first victory, and the impact it would have later.

That frustration was a sense—a *feeling*—that I had not delivered *real* justice to my client. You see, my client's legal fees alone—excluding "hidden" client costs like time and distraction—had consumed the disputed money stakes. (Not coincidentally, the same was true for both opposing counsel and their clients.) In fact, my fees were not just disproportionate to the stakes, they *dwarfed* them: Two weeks after the trial ended, I sat at my desk and added up my firm's legal bills over the life of the case (90% of which consisted of my time charged at my hourly rate) and compared that sum with how much money had been at stake. Even after writing off some of my time for tasks that had taken longer than I thought they should, I had spent about *$11,000* of my client's money, win or lose, while the money at stake—and what the case could have settled for—was *less than $6,000*.

> *That frustration was a sense—a* feeling—*that I had not delivered* real *justice to my client. You see, my client's legal fees alone—excluding "hidden" client costs like time and distraction—had consumed the disputed money stakes. (Not coincidentally, the same was true for both opposing counsel and their clients.) In fact, my fees were not just disproportionate to the stakes, they* dwarfed *them.*

Making matters worse, I knew that this business client had made less than $500 in net profit on the underlying product sale, and had costs of at least $4,500 to make and sell the product. If this exact "costs-of-doing-business" dispute and "victory" scenario were to play out in only 1 of every 1000 product sales—meaning that for each $500,000 in net profits, the company were to suffer an additional net loss of $11,000—its precious net profit margins would be lower by over 2%. And that was the *best case* scenario. Differences like that could bankrupt some companies, and in any event would rob *any* company of meaningful hard-earned profit.

Even knowing all this, my client was still delighted, because they had avoided suffering an unfair nuisance settlement and sought to build a reputation for not rolling over to extortion. (And no, this client was *not* just playing hardball with anyone who sued them, because I settled many cases for them when the facts were bad and settlement demands reasonable.) My senior mentors assured me, correctly at the time, that this was not in my power to change and that helping my client meet its legitimate goals should salve my guilt. But it still just didn't *feel* right.

Fortunately, since then, most of my cases involving such limited stakes have settled well before trial, at least in part because we lawyers and our clients came to recognize that the stakes didn't justify trial. On the plus side, this has reduced the number of times when clients have suffered the *injustice* of absurdly expensive legal process in order to vindicate a right cause. On the minus side, this *threat* of disproportionate costs in modest cases often has led me and countless other responsible lawyers to advise—or our clients grudgingly to accept— unfair compromises that frustrate legitimate rights and prevent truly just outcomes.

THE CHILD IN ME

That first post-trial frustration, and many of the pragmatic settlements I later obtained for clients, were at odds with my childhood ideals. I had not become a lawyer to purvey fake justice. I had become a lawyer to make a difference for good by helping people win real justice. That was my dream from as early as 5th grade, when I learned about and idolized Abraham Lincoln. I still remember that class assignment to draw a picture of what I wanted to be when I grew up. There I was, a fleshed-out stick figure standing in front of a judge's bench. Only later would I learn that lawyers could earn a good living in private civil litigation. And only *much* later would my farm upbringing—with its simple values about work, family, and bottom-line economics—drive my direction and career choices within the legal profession.

Looking back, I know I was lucky to have a happy, healthy childhood, stable family, and an inquisitive and analytical mind. I also was optimistic and fair-minded (if not overly idealistic) about what I expected from the world. Born in San Jose, California, on the last day of 1953, I was raised on my grandfather's family prune ranch in Santa Clara Valley when that area was known throughout the United States as the "Valley of Heart's Delight."

That same valley today is recognized worldwide as Silicon Valley. I grew up, not with the power and conveniences of digital technology, but with the simple beauty and wonder of fruit orchards and their windblown springtime blossom "storms." Mom and Dad were high school sweethearts who had married at 18. Our first home was a three-room, run-down shack on the prune ranch. I had two younger brothers with only 2½ years separating the three of us. The next eldest, Richard, was the most good-natured, kind, and generous of us. He would grow into the gentle giant and peacemaker of the family. Bill was intense, ambitious, and competitive—more like me—and our best athlete. No other children lived on the prune ranch, so early on we learned from each other how to compete, play with others, negotiate, and share.

My grandfather, his brothers, and my father—like all farmers— wore blue-collared work shirts and jeans and worked long dawn-to-dusk days. My first job was seasonally picking prunes at age 9, where I learned the meaning and value of hard, tedious work. Like any child, I hated it at the time. The only escape was playing softball every evening in a rough dirt field near our house, next to wooden tree-prop piles and stacks of trays for drying prunes. We played with the migrant Mexican and Mexican-American kids who were staying in the work camp across the field. When the movie *Sandlot* came out many years later, I realized it could almost have been written about us. Also, about that time, my brothers and I joined 4-H, because that's what rural California kids did. So I climbed the 4-H ladder of organizational training, personal achievement levels, and projects-learning (my favorite was entomology—the study of insects) until my late teens.

Along the way, Mom taught us to sing and persuaded us, as only mothers can, to learn to play musical instruments. Mine was the accordion. I learned to read and love music. Meanwhile, a string of caring teachers guided our early education, supplemented by Mom's love of books and Dad's math flash cards. I wanted to learn about everything, and found the work of learning to be stimulating. I became the best learner in each of my south San Jose public schools through high school.

The summer of my 13th year, Dad took me to work in his growing farm business in Gilroy. Six days per week for the next nine summers, I learned about harvesting garlic, cherries, pears, and bell peppers. I started in fields and orchards and later graduated to packing sheds, forklifts, and produce-hauling trucks of every size. In hindsight, that experience was immensely valuable in more ways than I can count, but at the time, its main teaching was that farming wasn't what I wanted to do with my life. I craved more variety, intellectual challenge, and my own path. School was a better fit, because I could supplement any tedious or boring classwork with an ambitious combination of immersive activities ranging from sports and student government to "nerdy" pastimes like singing, board games, acting, model building, and collecting (everything).

Fortunately, this all meant that my college applications were loaded with solid work experience and lots of extracurricular activities to go along with my good grades. I thus earned one of life's rewards for working hard and helping make my own luck when Stanford University admitted me in 1972 and graduated me with an A.B.[1] in Economics *with honors* in 1976. Over those four years, I had more fun, did more learning, experienced more outside-the-box adventures, and did more growing and lifelong friend-making, than any other time I can remember. Dad and Mom paid my room and board, but I had to pay half my tuition from my accumulated summer earnings. In addition to studying economics, I dabbled in psychology, human biology, philosophy, statistics, history, political science, and foreign language.

BRIEF

Lest you wonder, I was indeed in the Vietnam draft lottery in 1972, but the war was winding down and my number was higher than the threshold for the young men called to serve that year. With the same number the previous year before, I, too, would have been drafted. Whenever I meet veterans of that most difficult war, I am reminded how different my life could have been.

I played varsity volleyball, directed student musicals, spent six months attending school in Germany, and explored Europe on a cheap student "Interail" pass. Perhaps most importantly, I found in everything I did the humility that comes of realizing everyone has special skills and worth, and that there are many smarter and more talented people of all genders, ethnicities, and creeds.

Young life, however, was not always a bowl of the cherries that Dad grew and Mom turned into pies. Six months after I turned 21, brother Richard died in a solo car accident at about 2:00 a.m. after falling asleep at the wheel. He was exhausted from a late night of helping young 4-H kids pack and clean up from a weeklong summer camp in the Santa Cruz Mountains, where he had served as a senior counselor. The night before he left for camp, he had just returned from his first year at Cal Poly San Luis Obispo, so the two of us had gone out to catch up and see the latest Ray Harryhausen *Sinbad* movie (with its then-cutting-edge stop-action special effects). I had just returned from my European adventure sporting a beard and mustache, and Rich bore a set of facial scars from a run-in with a sliding glass door at his school dorm. The evening was one of reacquainting, sharing, appreciating, and looking forward. It was also the last time I saw him.

With Richard's death, the bubble burst. I suffered the deepest grief and sense of loss I've ever felt, *and until then didn't know I could feel*, as did the rest of the family. I know that we tend to sanctify loved ones who have passed, but Richard was a truly extraordinary human being. While a teenager, I remember telling Mom as we stood in our kitchen that the biggest difference between Richard and me was that I *choose* to do good because I'd figured out that it was *both* right and smarter in almost all situations, while it was simply Richard's nature. In any event, soon after his passing, I would stand witness to the slow and unexpected crumble of my parents' outwardly perfect marriage, while Bill and I would grow further apart for many years. Richard was our glue, and his death exposed our family's seams. Aside from the intensity of our feelings, the only good to come of it was that I vowed to become more like him. I'm still working on that.

FIRST CAREER—LAWYER WARRIOR

I attended law school at the University of California at Davis. If college helped me grow up and see farther out, law school focused me on legal knowledge and skills training. It also pointed me toward a career as a litigator in private practice: for the good I could do others; the competition and complex dramas that would forever challenge, engage, and teach me; the career I could build around my particular talents and passions; the livelihood I could make; and the control I hopefully could have over where and how I would raise my future family.

By the end of law school in May 1979, I had fared well, written and edited for the Law Review, and made more lifelong friends. I also strongly suspected I would not marry a lawyer. I didn't. I met Ginny while she was attending the Graduate School of Education at Davis and we married in September 1980. We raised two sons, Jason, born in 1984, and Tadon, born in 1986. Four decades later I am still blessed with the extraordinary good fortune of those events and the Gibraltar-like grounding and joy they bring me every day—now including four precious grandchildren. While this part of my story uses the fewest words, that is the only small thing about it.

Ambitions drove my early career. I wanted to become the best litigation attorney I could be, to work hard and advance myself in my firm, to succeed in marriage and family, and perhaps most naively, to make it on my own, unsheltered and unaided by Dad's steady climb to success and ultimate prominence as the nation's largest producer of fresh garlic, cofounder of the now famous Gilroy Garlic Festival, and Gilroy community benefactor. The independent path, of course, was the one he had taken in farming, choosing to strike out on his own at age 21. Twenty years later, he was deeply disappointed when I chose not to join him, but he has always maintained how proud he was of my ambition to rise on my own. Whether he truly felt that way, merely acquiesced, or succumbed to my too-lawyerly argument about having followed his lead, I will never know.

So I chose not to accept a good offer from a fine law firm in San Jose in large part because I needed more distance from my family's support system. Instead, I started my career in September 1979 at one of Los Angeles' top tier firms doing complex and high stakes litigation that included my preferred specialty, antitrust, for its interplay of law and economics. With this move, I gave up instant job security and the almost certain opportunity to help run a growing, industry-leading, and familiar business close to home.

Fortunately, I was *not a complete* idiot. About 1982, my brother and I got the chance to buy into Dad's business at a favorable price, in installments. Our uncle, a silent financial partner with my dad, wanted to diversify his risks by selling half of his shares, so we took the deal in a New York minute. I, for one, was very glad to stay connected to my farm roots and the family business in this way. Looking back, I'm certain that the reserve parachute these connections have represented over the course of my life has always helped me think clearer and act bolder.

My career as a civil litigation attorney spanned four decades, three law firms, and one move from Los Angeles back to Northern California's then-emerging Silicon Valley. That move occurred in late 1985, when I was hired to head litigation for a young technology law firm, so my lack of gray hair was not an impediment. That firm was acquired the next year by a major international law firm headquartered in New York. About 1988, I was elected an equity partner and, over time, was recruited into firm management roles.

The adventure into law firm management both cost and gained me much. My first role was as a member of the firm's worldwide partner compensation committee, then as managing partner of my office, and finally as managing partner for the Northern California region—three offices consisting of San Jose, Palo Alto, and San Francisco. In these roles, I learned the business side of private law firm practice, from the highs of overseeing profits and hiring staff to the lows of dealing with net losses and having to lay off good people in economic downturns. All in all, I gained invaluable experience and perspective, but I was consumed by work and not spending enough time with family.

Consequently, in 2005 I took early retirement from the New York firm in order to correct my absurd work-life imbalance. I joined a strong regional law firm in San Jose as "Of Counsel," a status I sought that would enable me to carry a lighter caseload, spend less time marketing, spend more time with my family, renew long-foregone personal passions like theater and music, and possibly pursue an emerging personal-professional passion. That plainly proved to be the right decision, as the next ten years became, overall, the most gratifying of my life.

Over my litigation career, I litigated hundreds of cases, in roles varying from junior member of large teams to solo and senior lead trial responsibility. The range of cases included antitrust and intellectual property (patent, trademark, and copyright) disputes of national import, a wide range of commercial business disputes (contract, warranty, fraud, interference, and the like), air crash and asbestos exposure liability suits, employment termination disputes, legal malpractice disputes, insurance coverage disputes, disputes over ownership and control of companies and nonprofit organizations including church communities, and disputes over estate fraud and breach of trust.

As is the case for many lawyers, the clients I worked for ran the gamut from major brand American and foreign corporations to dozens of relatively unknown and financially much smaller companies, organizations, and individuals. Most of the disputes were local, but many were international. The latter involved what I can only describe as an exotic overlay of cross-cultural legal systems, people, travel, and all the fascinating complexity and adventure that accompany them. Along the way, career highlights included early business trials (such as the one described at the beginning of this chapter), misdemeanor criminal prosecutions and trials while on loan to the Los Angeles District Attorney's

Office (to get jury trial experience), a hard-fought settlement for a small technology company against the nation's then-largest computer maker, a "bet-the-farm" jury verdict and community-celebrated defense victory for a deserving breakaway church community against a mother church bent on annihilation, a $6+ million plaintiff's jury verdict and *collected* settlement for the leading American manufacturer of fiberglass insulation cores against a Chinese mining and manufacturing conglomerate, occasional tangible expressions of client appreciation, admission to the U.S. Supreme Court, and a top Peer Review Rating for Ethical Standards and Legal Ability from national legal publisher Martindale-Hubbell (a genuinely unsolicited and peer-reviewed recognition). I also enjoyed occasionally serving as a neutral mediator, arbitrator, and settlement judge *pro tem* in Santa Clara County on a wide variety of cases. Of course, my career also had its losses, disappointments and other lowlights, though I choose to see each as ultimately delivering valuable learning.

On balance, I don't regret any of my thirty-seven years in litigation. They were challenging and fulfilling in every way I could have hoped, and they taught me the truths and led to the insights that I share in this book.

SECOND CAREER—MOVING ON AND GIVING BACK

About 2003, during my law office management period, two initially unrelated events changed everything. First, in order to learn how to *run* a business better—instead of simply work in one—I joined a local chapter of an international CEO peer organization called Vistage. Second, I took on the testing laboratory case described in Chapter 1 of this book.

Vistage enables business leaders to learn and share best practices in an environment of mutual confidence and trust. It's rare to have lawyers as members of Vistage CEO groups, so from day one I found myself surrounded by about fifteen experienced entrepreneurs and CEOs—all glad for the opportunity to occasionally share their legal frustrations and nightmares and ask for my first-blink impressions on pending legal challenges. Meanwhile, my laboratory testing case was moving along and becoming increasingly frustrating to my client and me, as we had both hoped for an early settlement before legal fees and delays consumed the value of the dispute. It was only natural, then, that I eventually shared with my fellow Vistage members my own frustrations with my client's situation and the justice system from which I admittedly made a lucrative living. This in turn led to a series of conversations about what business people think of our justice system (too expensive and wasteful of everyone's time), what they think is responsible for that (greedy lawyers and excessive process), and what might be done about it (focused and limited discovery, reduced delays, and less maneuvering).

Something snapped in me. I began analyzing legal bills—mine and others. I interviewed colleagues and clients to confirm whether my experience was typical and ask what might be done to reduce expense and waste without sacrificing the quality of justice. I ran scenarios in which I imagined rules *limiting* formal discovery, jury trials, formalized pleadings, briefs, and confrontational hearings. I considered not only the potential savings from these rule changes but also their practicalities, impracticalities, and likely impacts on the overall quality, perception, and reliability of outcomes. It didn't take long before an answer began to emerge: No matter what rule changes I made, if three conditions are met, the parties routinely will fail to earn real, economically rational justice, regardless of who officially wins or loses. Those conditions are:

- Money stakes are limited (i.e., likely to be mostly or entirely consumed by legal fees and related costs)
- Competing lawyers drive the action
- There's no early settlement.

However, as soon as I took the battling lawyers out of the driver's seat, the potential emerged for an efficient and focused search for truth and a reliably fair and economic outcome.

> *I began analyzing legal bills—mine and others. I interviewed colleagues and clients to confirm whether my experience was typical and ask what might be done to reduce expense and waste without sacrificing the quality of justice.*

In short, my "Eureka!" moment was that the ultimate obstacle appeared to be me! Well, more accurately, me, my fellow litigators, and our adversarial system. One of my key findings was that *over 2/3* of litigation lawyers' recorded time is typically spent on tasks that are *not* focused on learning the truth about the underlying events and the law that applies to them. Instead, litigators spend most of their time communicating, coordinating, scheduling, objecting, waiting, strategizing, maneuvering, anticipating, accommodating, writing, editing, preparing, explaining, excusing, and arguing. *The time we spend actually investigating what happened and researching what law applies is modest by comparison.* **Figure 3** graphically depicts this simple yet key insight.

FIGURE 3 Why Litigation Costs So Much: Lawyers Spend 2/3 or More of Their Time on Process-Focused Activity.

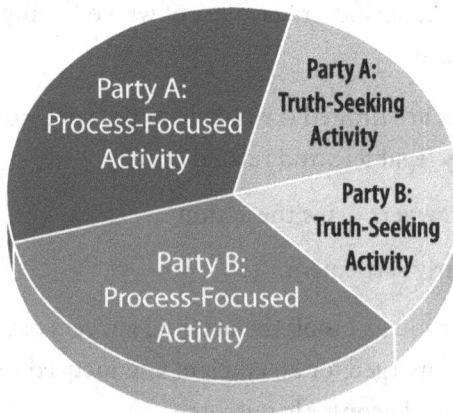

But change the approach and many of the most time-consuming tasks are *not necessary*. That revelation launched me on a mission to design a better way. At the strong urging of my Vistage colleagues, I later founded a new business dedicated to this mission, which I named *Just Resolve*.

In 2005, I left my international law firm of twenty years to explore and develop this better way, and moved to a local law firm that even encouraged my sideline—so long as it didn't distract from the quality of my work for clients. Perhaps it was a mistake to continue to practice law during what amounted to the initial R&D phase of the new business, as it divided my attention and energy, but I'm a litigator at heart and have always loved serving clients zealously on the legal battlefield. I also felt that it would help both pursuits to keep a hand in each for a while.

I knew something else too: I was uniquely positioned to pursue this mission not only because of my mix of farm, business, and legal experience and perspectives but also because I enjoyed financial security at this late stage in my career, thanks in no small part to the family farm business to which I owed so much. This perspective eventually led me to make another life-changing decision: I accepted Dad's and Bill's offer to become General Counsel of our farm business on a part-time basis. This gave me the opportunity not only to give back to the farm but also to begin to test—in real case evaluations and negotiations—the usefulness, power, and economy of the more principled and less adversarial approach to resolving differences that underlay my new mission. As of this writing, I have been doing that for about seven years.

It is in this context that in 2015 I insanely, but knowingly, stepped off that comfortable plateau of law firm practice and dropped into an abyss devoted to an uncertain and audacious future intent on making everyday civil justice better, faster, and cheaper.

CHAPTER SUMMARY

- My upbringing and experience may help you evaluate the innovation that this book champions.

- I grew up on an orchard farm in Northern California and worked for my Dad's garlic produce ranch full-time every summer from ages 13 to 22. I later bought into that business and today am its General Counsel.

- I did well in school, and along with my two younger brothers loved sports and singing. I also enjoyed student leadership and "nerdy" pastimes like board games, collecting, model building, and acting.

- I was lucky enough not to be drafted in the Vietnam lottery and instead went to college and law school. I graduated college with honors in Economics, played varsity volleyball, directed student musicals, and studied abroad. In law school, I wrote and edited for the Law Review.

- My middle brother tragically died in a freak auto accident in 1975. My parents split up less than two years later.

- I pursued a career in business litigation, climbing the big private law firms ladder, first in Los Angeles and later in Northern California. I rose to partner and later regional managing partner of a prominent NY-based international law firm. I am married over forty years and blessed with two sons, daughters-in-law, and four grandchildren.

- I joined a CEO peer group in order to better manage the business of my law firm. Soon after, I began studying the recurring problem of too-expensive justice in everyday cases. I also became increasingly disenchanted with law firm work-life imbalance, so I took an early retirement benefit to work as "Of Counsel" with a fine regional law firm who allowed my sideline exploration into uneconomic litigation and search for potential solutions.

- In the course of my 42-year legal career, I've actively litigated many hundreds of cases across dozens of industries and legal fields, including antitrust, intellectual property, vendor, purchaser, partner, employment, legal services, insurance, and pro bono disputes. I've also served as a neutral mediator, arbitrator, and settlement judge "pro tem" in the local superior court. I have enjoyed many career wins and other highlights, suffered disappointing losses, and earned a nationally published top peer review rating for legal competence and ethics.

- My study of too-expensive justice revealed that over 2/3 of the recorded time battling lawyers typically spend in litigation is spent on tasks that are *not* focused on learning the truth about the underlying events and the law that applies to them. This discovery, depicted in **Figure 3**, exposed a primary obstacle to real justice in everyday disputes. It also pointed toward the solution.

"Ms. Burney, do we have anything on right and wrong?"

CHAPTER 3

THE LAW: HOW DID WE GET HERE?

PART ONE

In the Beginning . . .

Humans have been litigating for almost as long as we've been arguing. Whether early arguments were over a hide or a choice spot in the cave, our earliest human ancestors routinely faced situations requiring dispute resolution—no doubt sometimes involving threats or acts of violence and readily weaponized tools like sticks and rocks. It couldn't have taken long for members of the clan to realize that engaging in and tolerating violent means of resolution threatened the security and prosperity of all.

Less mutually destructive solutions were needed. Consequently—whether dictated by a clan strongman, or conducted by a chieftain, revered wise man, or tribal council—there were prehistoric trials and mediations of all sorts. As we've evolved and progressed, our disputes have become more complex and our methods of resolution more sophisticated. We've grown beyond the thrown gauntlet and pistols at dawn, and we now duel by pleading and arbitration—less bloody, but still as contentious.

Before we present a better path forward for the here and now, it's helpful to take a step back and look at how law and litigation developed. We don't have to be historians to know that where we've been will inform the way forward. That said, if you're pressed for time, feel free to skip ahead to Part Two of this chapter.

EARLIEST LEGAL CODES—A MIX OF REASON AND SUPERSTITION

The earliest known legal codes are thought to come from China between four and five thousand years ago. Emperor Fuxi, who according to Chinese legend exercised mind control over animals and the weather, is given credit for the creation of the first Chinese law code. The key element in his code was balance. He felt that maintaining societal and natural balance through the prevention and punishment of criminal deeds was paramount. Superstition played a major role in the early application of law (much as it did in everything else). For example, the markings on tortoise shells were believed to help divine justice.[1]

While considerably more recent, Mesopotamian contributions to legal history are better known to Westerners. Between 2350 BC and

2050 BC, societies in the Fertile Crescent region of the Middle East began codifying law with "if . . . then" statements, such as "[i]f any one break a hole into a house (with the intent to steal), he shall be put to death before that hole and be buried." The establishment of the king as an appointee of the gods, and therefore the arbiter of the law, is another early development in the Mesopotamian legal codes, as is the concept of testimony given under oath.[2]

The first recorded legal decision comes from this region in 1850 BC. The trial concerned the death of a temple employee, whose wife was accused of murder along with three men. The wife brought witnesses who backed up her claims of spousal abuse. In light of this evidence, the wife was spared the death penalty, although the other three defendants were executed in front of the victim's house.[3] This decision appears to have introduced the notions of "extenuating circumstances" and, dare I say it, a crude precursor to "credit for time served."

Arguably the most famous historical legal code is that of Babylonian emperor Hammurabi, which dates to 1750 BC. From Hammurabi we get both an "eye for eye" and the origin of the word "villain." As to the latter, a class equivalent to serfs was then called "villeins," a term that survived into the Middle Ages via Latin adoption. These *villeins* eventually gave rise to the term *villain*, along with the connotation of wrongdoer not originally associated with it.[4]

Perhaps most notably for the subsequent development of litigation, Hammurabi's code placed a high value on witness testimony and the opportunity to discover evidence. For example, to exonerate oneself from a charge of possession or sale of stolen merchandise, one had to bring the merchant into court to testify to lawful sale, and defendants were allowed a six-month period to investigate and produce witnesses. Hammurabi's code also represents a major expansion of civil law, including the introduction of slander laws, the establishment of uniform compensation rates for services and losses, and provisions for spousal support, custody rights, and regulation of adoption.[5]

It's noteworthy that none of these earliest legal codes appear to contemplate the creation and recognition of lawyer advocates—although we may easily imagine that throughout time, persons accused of wrongdoing may have relied, when permitted, on someone else to advise or speak for them.

TWELVE ROMAN TABLES AND MAGNA CARTA— FOUNDATIONS OF MODERN LAW

Around 450 BC, a plebian tribune, Gaius Terentilius Harsa, urged the Roman Senate to adopt an extraordinary innovation to promote balance and peace in Roman society: He argued that *all* Roman citizens, patrician and plebian alike, should enjoy the equal protection of laws under a uniform written code. An anonymous collection of Roman authors subsequently assembled a set of laws and recorded them on twelve bronze tablets, which became known as the *12 Roman Tables*.[6] From these laws grew such modern Western legal concepts as perjury, slander, punitive damages, witness subpoenas, inheritance and estate law, and punishment for corruption. Most importantly, from this point on, Roman law was written and judges were charged with interpreting and applying it to cases before them. While English common law would eventually splinter off from its Roman ancestry, modern Western civil law can trace much of its heritage back to these twelve bronze tablets.

There were many interesting developments in legal history after the 12 Roman Tables, but the next comparable event deserving a nod here is Magna Carta, almost eight centuries later.

Runnymede, England is a lush meadow and river basin along the Thames River some twenty miles west of London. No buildings that existed on June 15, 1215 (when King John signed Magna Carta), survive, but the Ankerwycke Yew, a 1,400-year-old tree under which the document apparently was sealed, still stands. Almost 300 acres are preserved around it in dedication to the occasion, along with twelve bronze chairs representing jurors, decorated with symbolic represen-tations of the struggles therein addressed. Even the American Bar Association erected a memorial to Magna Carta in 1957 bearing the inscription: "To commemorate Magna Carta, symbol of Freedom Un-der Law."[7]

What took place that late Spring day in 1215 was a monumental change in the evolution of law. For the first time in history, a mon-arch who claimed that his right to the throne came directly from God agreed that he, in fact, was not above the rule of law, nor was he the ultimate source of law over the people. Magna Carta was the first bill of rights for the people, and established that the law was a concept great-er than ruler or government. Despite the fact that King John sealed the document under the threat of rebellion from English barons, the document survived and became the primary foundation for English common law.

In the United States, we similarly trace our common law tradi-tion and right to due process of law to Chapter 39 of Magna Carta:

> No free man shall be seized or imprisoned, or stripped of
> his rights or possessions, or outlawed or exiled, or deprived
> of his standing in any other way, nor will we proceed with
> force against him, or send others to do so, except by the
> lawful judgement of his equals or by the law of the land.[8]

In this single sentence, we see the underpinnings for trial by jury, prohibitions against illegal imprisonment, search, and seizure, and the later American Declaration of Independence, Constitution, and Bill of Rights. American law owes a paramount debt to this great document.

THE BUMPY RISE OF LAWYERS

First Lawyers—Or Not?

About 530 BC in Athens, the Greek poet Solon was appointed medi-ator for disputes between serfs and landlords. He created a set of laws for serf and landlord alike that included the right of representation for those unable to represent themselves, and an appeals court. Until then, if you had a case to bring or an accusation against which you needed to defend, you represented yourself. These laws did not authorize lawyers as we know them today. Instead, they permitted representation only by a friend who agreed to appear on a party's behalf without pay. In practice, the ban on payment for representation was often circumvented and the designation of "friend" was stretched, but the Athenian orators who appeared in court for litigants could not advertise or promote themselves as legal representation for hire.[9] Apparently, even then there was concern that hired advocacy could have a dark side and lead to "excessive" legal fees.

> *The Athenian orators who appeared in court for litigants could not advertise or promote themselves as legal representation for hire. Apparently, even then there was concern that hired advocacy could have a dark side and lead to "excessive" legal fees.*

In the 1st century AD, Emperor Claudius of Rome lifted the ban against paying for representation in the courts; however, the most that could be charged was ten thousand sesterces. Considering that Roman house prices varied between a half million and two-and-a-half million sesterces, a Roman lawyer had to hustle to make his mortgage payment. In fact, the Roman poet and satirist Juvenal (who gave rise to the term *juvenile*) once commented that being a lawyer was a less profitable profession than that of charioteer and there was no money in it.[10]

Despite the low wages, Claudius' recognition of legal advocates led to the formal organization of the profession. By the 4th century, the lawyer as a professional had solidified his presence in Roman society.

Before a lawyer—a *juris consult*—could argue in court, he had to enroll on the bar list of that court and could argue only in that one court. Although the first school dedicated to the study of law was founded in Beirut about 250 AD, it wasn't until the year 460 that Emperor Leo required all lawyers to obtain testimonials from their teachers—giving lawyers their first bar examination. By the 5th century, Roman law school was a regulated four-year course of study.[11]

Middle Age Crisis

In the Middle Ages, the legal profession all but collapsed. The fall of the Roman Empire and conquest of central Europe by Germanic tribes—whose tribal customs included trial by combat—decimated the profession and caused upheaval in the concepts of property rights, personal freedoms, and the administration of law, which led to a breakdown of the advanced, regulated court system created by the Roman Empire. Not until some priests began devoting their careers to Canon Law for the Catholic Church around the year 1140 did lawyers begin to make a comeback.[12]

This isn't to say that people living under the rule of Germanic tribal leaders had *no* right of representation. A vassal who appeared before the court benefitted from the presence of his lord to lend credence to the vassal's case. Friends and relatives were permitted to accompany any person who presented or defended a case, and the participant was allowed to confer with those friends and relatives prior to presenting his testimony. Eventually, this right expanded to include a *forespeka*, or "pleader," to help the party make his case. This role differs from that of a lawyer, as the *forespeka* was not permitted to argue the merits of the case or make legal arguments. The *forespeka* was limited to merely telling the court what the party involved wished to say.[13]

Not until the advent of the Germanic *torn* did lawyers see a resurgence in Europe. Germanic and Anglo-Saxon tribes regularly held regional meetings called *torn*. If a person could not attend the meeting, they were entitled to be *"attorned"* by sending a representative. The French adopted the word as *attornee* and later Latinized it as *attorna-tus*. While some accounts of the role played by these early attorneys have them acting fully on behalf of absent persons, others indicate that the job was more akin to a mere messenger, until the reign of Henry II (1154–1189).[14]

As the profession rose again, it seemed to so do under a guise closer to the *attorn* of Germanic tribal gatherings than of the *juris consults* of the Roman Empire. Norman attorneys in France and England could only appear on behalf of their client if their client was not present in court. If the client was present, the judge could ignore the attorney and the client was required to represent himself. In order to remove his attorney, the client need merely show up and make his wishes known to the court. At some point, in Normandy, the power to remove one's attorney was revoked, and the attorney was required to resign voluntarily before the client could represent himself or appoint other counsel. This requirement does not appear in English records where clients have retained the nearly unfettered right to appoint and dismiss representation. Eventually, an educational requirement of five years of legal study (later reduced to three in England), and admittance to the bar, became prerequisite to entitlement to practice.[15] From this point, the presence of the attorney in society was cemented, and the profession grew in size and scope.

Curiously, lawyers have been maligned nearly since their reappearance in Europe. In 1381, English peasants revolted against perceived injustice in taxation.[16] At that time, it was common practice for English nobility to enlist lawyers as enforcers of the collection of taxes, often resulting in beheadings of non-payers and so, not too surprisingly, earning lawyers a quite negative reputation. In fact, it's to this reputation that Shakespeare addresses the famous and oft-quoted line from *Henry VI*, "The first thing we do, let's kill all the lawyers."[17]

It's a bit sad, but hardly surprising, that some contemporary lawyers have seen fit to twist Shakespeare's famous lawyer joke—one lamenting lawyers' negative reputations at the time—into a self-serving message about the societal good lawyers do to protect citizens and truth against tyranny and injustice.[18] Completely ignoring the historical context in which Shakespeare wrote and the plain intention of his comical reference, the lawyer-whitewashed versions claim that Shakespeare actually intended to commend lawyers, "explaining" that the evil character who utters this line in *Henry VI* is imagining a utopia in which there are no lawyers to prevent royal abuses of power, when in truth it was the evil that lawyers were then perceived to be doing on behalf of those in power that prompted Shakespeare's literary suggestion.[19] In all events, debunking the spin here serves as both a lesson in and illustration of the dangers of overly creative lawyering at its wishful thinking worst.

As with much of Shakespeare's work, his jab at lawyers may have been a reflection of the legal climate in England at the time the play was written. In 1605, fourteen years after scholars believe *Henry VI* was penned, the resurgence of the legal profession had become a pestilence, and the English Parliament passed *An Act to Reform the Multitudes and Misdemeanors of Attornies and Solicitors at Law and to Avoid Unnecessary Suits and Charges in Law.*[20] The statute addresses two problems Parliament perceived with lawyers at the beginning of the 17th century. The first was excessive fees and unnecessary demands made on clients by attorneys. In order to prevent fraudulent charges, attorneys were required to have their bills reviewed by the court and a "ticket" verified before they could present the bill to their client. The ticket required the attorney specify the number of times he appeared before the court on his client's behalf. The second perceived problem was that there were too many attorneys, and many of those were unfit for the profession. The statute therefore also required that all new attorneys demonstrate their skill and ethical behavior before they could practice independently of a supervising attorney, two prerequisites still required in some manner of all modern lawyers.

With the inauguration of professional regulation came a new class of lawyer: the barrister, a legal professional specifically licensed to appear in court on behalf of a client. In the United States, only South Carolina still requires a separate license for attorneys who wish to argue court cases, and the term barrister is not used. In England, however, the barrister class created a layer of separation between those legal professionals who advised clients on general matters (now generally referred to as solicitors), and those who were admitted to the bar. As late as 1650 in England, no single method of legal education and training was codified into law, allowing the apprentice method to continue its dominance.[21]

Colonial American Lawyers

The 17th century is important to the development of American litigation because it's then that the English colonists began to arrive in North America, bringing their legal traditions with them. Jamestown, Virginia, the first successful English settlement in North America, erected its first structures in 1607, although it wasn't until 1619 that a representative British government was formed there. In 1620, the *Mayflower* reached Cape Cod, Massachusetts.[22] Other than a vague reference to lawyers intervening on John Smith's behalf in Jamestown, the meaning of which is uncertain, there are no records that suggest that a trained attorney was aboard the ships that first landed in what is now Virginia and Massachusetts. This doesn't preclude the presence of early colonists having education or training in the law, but no one whose profession was listed as attorney appears in the passenger lists.

Nevertheless, there was definitely rule of law in the colonies, mostly granted by charters from the king. Plymouth appears to be an exception with its colonists publishing their first code in 1638 as a combination of English law and Judeo-Christian law.[23] In either event, crimes were punished by authoritative bodies and disputes among residents were resolved by "judges," so the presence of government authority and the promulgation of law in the colonies begs only the question: Who served as their attorneys?

The answer is at least twofold. First, trained attorneys eventually did come from England at various points, some staying only temporarily in the colonies. Second, a class of self-identified attorneys (more accurately men with various degrees of literacy and legal training) rose out of necessity and established themselves as a profession. Often these men functioned as members of the colonial governments, from councilmen to treasurers and even governors.

The vast majority of attorneys who appeared in colonial courts were men, although there are records, particularly in Maryland, of women appearing before the bar. Arguably the most remarkable and famous of these women was Mistress Margaret Brent.[24] In 1648, Brent appeared before the colonial governor of Maryland and requested a voice and a vote in the governmental assembly. Ms. Brent was not without cause to make her request, as she had already established herself as an able law practitioner, appearing in court as attorney, plaintiff, and defendant numerous times. Brent was also executrix or legal representative for some two dozen estates, and owned property in her own right.

Revolutionary Change in America

Informed by their classical educations and the philosophy of the Enlightenment, and fueled by abuses suffered at the hands of the English monarchy, the Framers of the U.S. Constitution and Bill of Rights in the late 1780s focused on the rights of citizens. This perspective led to founding a then-extraordinary form of government, a republican democracy. Most important to the topic of justly resolving conflicts, the new federal government established the judiciary as a third, coequal, and independent branch of government, and explicitly promised due process of law in the courts, the right to trial by jury in criminal and common law disputes alike, and the right to legal counsel.

Early American universities chartered the first American law schools following the Revolutionary War. The College of William and Mary lays claim to beginning law instruction in 1779, but because its law school closed during the Civil War and did not reopen until 1922, Harvard University School of Law, founded in 1817, claims to be the oldest continuous law school in the United States.[25]

Raising the Bar

In 1878, just over a century after the Revolution, and thirteen years following the Civil War's end, the American Bar Association (ABA) was formed in Saratoga Springs, New York.[26] Connecticut lawyer Simeon Baldwin is credited as the driving force for the creation of the self-governing body that today guides regulation of much of the legal profession in the United States. The growth and import of the American Bar Association is remarkable, if for no other reason than only seventy-five attorneys of the 600 Baldwin invited attended that first formational meeting. Perhaps symbolic of the ABA's mission to *assure meaningful access to justice for all persons*, the original gavel used by the first eighty ABA presidents from 1878 until 1956 was a humble wooden carpenter's mallet.[27]

Today, the ABA claims to be one of the world's largest professional organizations with over 400,000 members. Membership is not restricted to lawyers and law students, but to anyone interested in American law and the legal profession. One of the ABA's most important functions is accrediting law schools which educate American lawyers. The ABA also provides oversight, ethical directives and guidelines, discipline, and continuing education.[28]

The development of codified law and the rise of the legal profession have come a long way from the early days of tortoise shell markings and *forespeka*. For better or worse, the law and lawyers have married to create a complex system of justice. Some efforts in America to align the interests of law, lawyers, and justice have succeeded, while others have not. Consequently, we continue to work the challenges from many angles, as Part Two reveals.

PART TWO

From Litigation to Alternative Dispute Resolution

PAYING THE BILL

From early colonial days through the middle of the 20th century, attorneys charged for services on a project or "flat fee" basis. Consequently, legal fees in lawsuits tended to reflect and be proportional to value actually conferred. In some colonies, legislatures went so far as to regulate the fees that clients paid for legal services. In others, attorneys could determine their own fees but were still paid on a flat fee basis, with complaints of high or excessive fees investigated by colonial authorities.[29]

After the Revolution, states often capped fees. Contingency fees and retainers grew in popularity after the Civil War and accelerated after 1920. A New York law firm began tracking attorney hours by case matter in 1945 as a way to determine profit margins. By the late 1950s, the capped-fee system was on its way out and an ABA publication entitled *The 1958 Lawyer and His 1938 Dollar* asserted that attorneys were making less than the going rate for other comparatively educated professions, namely dentists.[30] Fees based on billable hours thereafter grew in popularity, albeit slowly, until 1975 when the Supreme Court ruled that it was a violation of antitrust laws for bar associations to set minimum fees.[31] Since then, billable hours have become the norm for legal services charges that are not contingency-based.

SEE YOU IN COURT

The earliest historical records evidencing alternative (i.e., *non-court*) forums for civil dispute resolution date back to Mesopotamian kingdoms almost two millennia before the birth of Christ. In ancient Greece in 350 BC, Aristotle wrote about the flexibility of arbitration to be more fair and "equitable" to litigants than courts, which look only to the strict confines of written law.[32] Seventeenth century court records from both sides of the Atlantic also report use of alternative processes much like today's mediation and arbitration.[33] Creativity also has occurred in *judicial* procedure. From early in the history of the United States, local court rules have varied from state to state and county to county, even after the federal government established the federal courts and began encouraging procedural uniformity in all American courts.[34]

By 1911, the ABA launched a national movement to adopt a uniform code for court rules. In 1938, the Federal Rules of Civil Procedure ("FRCP") were adopted and became the law of the land in all federal courts.[35] Amended periodically, the FRCP and similar sets of procedural rules at the state level strive to deliver fair and transparent judicial process throughout the country. That level of process, however, comes at extraordinary costs in time and legal fees, which can quickly eclipse the stakes in everyday litigation. This unfortunate reality has given rise to an entire industry and a number of alternative processes generally named Alternative Dispute Resolution, or "ADR." The best-known and most widespread of these ADR methods is arbitration.

ARBITRATION: LITIGATION IN SHEEP'S CLOTHING?

In the wake of the global economic depression known as The Panic of 1873, the Great Railway Strike of 1877 led Congress, after using troops to break some of the strike lines, to enact various legislative responses. These included the so-called Arbitration Act of 1888, granting the federal government the power to create arbitration panels to investigate and settle labor disputes on a more practical and expedited basis than the courts.[36] Unfortunately, the Act restricted the panels to nonbinding awards, and has been judged an abject failure based upon its single test, the 1894 Pullman strike, which ended only through the intervention of armed federal soldiers. Despite this disappointing record, the 1888 law led to more effective arbitration legislation and eventually the National Labor Relations Act.

While these early arbitration laws governed only labor disputes, by 1925 Congress recognized the potential application of arbitration to other legal disputes and passed the Federal Arbitration Act.[37] This Act, signed by President Coolidge, provides for:

- A contractually agreed quasi-judicial process
- Private and binding awards in place of public judgments
- Oversight and decisions by arbitrators, single or in panels, in place of judges
- Awards convertible into generally unappealable, enforceable judgments if needed
- No requirement to follow strict rules of federal or state courtroom procedure or evidence—granting administering organizations and arbitrators much flexibility in the interests of efficiency

One year later, the American Arbitration Association ("AAA") was established with a mission to foster arbitration as a wide-scale, private, less formal, and therefore more efficient alternative to lawsuits,[38] much along the lines of Aristotle's observations over 2,400 years ago.

SIDEBAR

Class Actions

Class actions are lawsuits brought in the name of representative member(s) of a group of people to right a claimed wrong that all members of the group may have suffered so similarly that common issues and proof outweigh individual differences for purposes of the efficient administration of justice. Most states have statutory schemes enabling such lawsuits.

Views differ widely inside and outside the legal profession over the net social good or harm done by class actions. Proponents—usually class action attorneys and advocates for historically disadvantaged groups like labor, consumers, and the poor—argue powerfully that class actions enable individuals to obtain justice and compel better corporate behavior towards them in situations where cost and other factors would otherwise prevent these achievements.

Opponents—usually businesses—decry the growing industry of opportunistic lawyers who recruit angry and malleable clients to pursue often questionable claims that, because they purport to represent others similarly situated, are more expensive and time-consuming to defend than prudent business sense dictates—forcing extortion-like settlements. There's considerable truth in both viewpoints. On the subject of class arbitrations, it's worth noting here that, because agreements to arbitrate a dispute are contractual and favored under the law, the courts so far have tended to respect contractual waivers of representative/class claims in arbitration clauses, thus assuring that individuals must each bring their own claims.[39]

Much of that potential improvement in efficiency, however, has been offset by increasingly lawsuit-like procedural and discovery rules favored by attorneys. Unfortunately, there are few in the arbitration system tasked to resist this backward slippage into familiar (expensive) process. Neutral arbitrators, their sponsoring organizations, and even the legislators who create arbitration rules are themselves mostly attorneys. Consequently, the foxes guard the henhouse and are ill-equipped to make the argument that neither fairness nor justice are advanced when more process rights and advocacy make legal costs absurd. Thus, arbitration too often has become *"mini-me"* litigation—just another expensive, advocate-driven, time-consuming, and open-ended process that consumes the financial stakes well before issuing an award. For instance, the AAA in 2003 promulgated its own rules for "class arbitrations" that mirror, for better or worse, much of the formalism, opportunity, and consequences of class action lawsuits.[40]

Other arbitration providers have similar sets of rules, although many recently have begun crafting simpler rules that the parties may choose for simpler disputes. In recent years, over-burdened courts have begun encouraging and sometimes ordering parties to engage in nonbinding arbitration as a condition to being set for trial. Nevertheless, most arbitrations are conducted privately and are intended to be a simpler, less costly alternative to court, so they conclude with a binding, enforceable, unappealable decision.

MEDIATION: ARBITRATION'S LESS DECISIVE SIBLING

Moving down the scale away from formality and finality, the next popular level of ADR is mediation.

Historically, mediation also traces its roots to ancient Greece, although some historical records indicate that Phoenician merchants practiced mediation, and that Buddhism and Confucianism embraced mediation from their inceptions.[41]

Modern mediation is similar to both arbitration and courtroom litigation in its reliance on *adversarial process*—i.e., a competition between opposing attorney teams who investigate, prepare, and choose what to present to a neutral professional who plays a relatively passive and reactive role, such as a judge, referee, or facilitator. However, mediation is very different from arbitration and litigation in the following particulars:

- It can take place at any time, before or after formal claim-filing, investigation, discovery, even trial.

- Presentations are typically made in written briefs with selected exhibits prepared by attorneys who may submit whatever they wish. There's no judge, formal hearing, rules of evidence, or direct or cross-examination of witnesses.

- The mediation itself is a settlement negotiation consisting of a set of confidential and informal meetings, often conducted shuttle-diplomacy style, attended by opposing attorneys and clients, and facilitated by an active neutral mediator. The mediator's role is not to make a decision, but rather to explore and promote a settlement acceptable to all parties. Because it's *not* a binding process that concludes with a judicially enforceable decision, it may fail to resolve the dispute.

- To reach resolution, all parties must negotiate in good faith, compromise, and ultimately sign a written settlement agreement.

Mediated disputes that don't settle may advance to arbitration or trial in court. Mediation often is recommended for disputes in which at least one party has a high emotional investment that may be the primary obstacle to resolution. Consequently, this is a method frequently used in family law matters, but now also increasingly in disputes of all kinds, as the risks and many high costs of litigation otherwise loom. It has the potential and attraction, if it works, to prevent or stop future legal costs of litigation in their tracks. The drawback of mediation is the lack of finality in the process: If it doesn't work, i.e., the parties don't reach agreement, it has just added to the overall time and expense of eventual resolution.

SIDEBAR

Case Study—Competitors' Mediation
Better Late than Never

A recent case in Northern California provides a classic example of the dilemmas, misuse, and waste inherent in almost all modest-sized business lawsuits, while it also reveals the good, bad, and ugly of mediation.

A reputable transport and storage company hired away one, and then a second, new sales person from an aggrieved competitor. Both new employees swore they had taken nothing confidential from their old jobs. Immediately after each was hired, the competitor retained litigation counsel who sent cease and desist letters warning the former employees against using any of the competitor's product pricing or customer information, and then filed suit against them before any meaningful conversation, information exchange, or demands took place. Refusing to be intimidated, the new employer committed to defend and indemnify the new employees and hired litigation counsel to handle their cases.

No one on the new employer's side estimated what the defense of the cases could cost. No one suggested mediation or any other conciliatory process, because neither company knew enough yet about the actual facts to assess how much the case was worth. There was also reason for the defense camp to believe that the competitor's strategy was more about inflicting punishing costs on its rival than it was about getting justice.

Both sides decided to fight fire with fire. Extensive procedural maneuvering ensued while records were demanded. The parties sparred over what confidential information might be involved and how not to reveal to the other side what they each had and knew. Consequently, over the next nine months, the new employer incurred over $700,000 in legal fees, with no end to the suit in sight. Indeed, not only was there no scheduled trial date, but at that point not a single deposition of a witness had been taken by either side. Even the competitor, whose attorney was working on a partial contingency basis (meaning he would be paid largely from any monies recovered), also began feeling the heat of legal fees and time invested that threatened to dwarf any realistic recovery in the case.

Meanwhile, in the midst of the process, the new employer, to his considerable disappointment, learned that one of the two new hires had lied about not taking the competitor's customer data. While the competitor did not yet know this and had no information suggesting it had occurred, the defense team quickly investigated and found that the potential loss to the competitor was no more than $20,000, even using worst case assumptions about the offending employee's possible use of the purloined information (which he insisted he had not done in light of the original cease and desist demand). However, the implications to the final outcome of the case were great.

The besieged new employer knew he had to stop the bleeding, so he replaced his California defense litigation counsel with his longtime Colorado business attorney and the parties agreed to mediate. A mediator was retained and both sides submitted briefs and exhibits. At mediation, the competitor's inflated initial demand was $600,000, and the employer's low-ball initial offer was $20,000. The case settled for $180,000, which was well less than what the employer estimated he would pay in further legal fees to try the case and potentially lose by way of an adverse verdict. (The employer's CEO would also later estimate the value of his own lost time by multiplying the number of hours he was distracted from work by an hourly rate based on his salary. That additional hidden cost exceeded $500,000!)

When the dust cleared, the defendant employer's total legal fees alone were $840,000. This dwarfed any reasonable estimate of the case's worth, whether $20,000 or the $180,000 settlement. In short, small fortunes were spent, a lot of time was lost or wasted, neither side won anything, and only the lawyers made money.

NEUTRAL EVALUATION AND SETTLEMENT CONFERENCES

Rounding out the historical context underlying today's civil justice gap are two more methods of ADR: **Neutral Evaluations** and **Settlement Conferences**. These too are common, nonbinding ADR methods that may be required by courts or agreed to by parties in specific circumstances.

Neutral evaluation is exactly what its name suggests. All parties, almost always acting through their attorneys, bring their arguments and evidence to a neutral party whose role is to assess and evaluate the strengths and weaknesses of the opposing presentations. This is particularly valuable for technical disputes where an expert evaluator can be used, as the opinion of the evaluator can be a springboard for negotiations toward settlement.

A similar type of neutral evaluation is a method common in large construction projects where disputes of certain kinds are likely to arise and delays can be financially disastrous to all involved. This method makes use of a Dispute Resolution Board ("DRB") that includes subject matter experts on whom the parties agree at the outset of the project and then compensate as shared overhead to monitor the project's progress. If a dispute arises, the experts investigate immediately and recommend a solution. The potential benefits of this approach include speed and potential avoidance of legal costs and confrontation. However, the experts' recommendation is usually only advisory, their pre-dispute retainers are overhead that is too high for limited stakes projects, and the approach isn't feasible where the range of potential disputes and needed subject matter expertise cannot be reliably predicted.

Settlement conferences are usually conducted with a judge or other assigned settlement officer, not to debate evidence or law, but to discuss potential settlement. The judge/officer can assist in evaluating likely evidence; however, the focus of the conference is on the potential for and terms of settlement. Often settlement conferences take place just days before the start of trials in court. In these conferences, the neutral settlement judge/officer does not render an opinion or a make a judgment, but helps the parties negotiate toward an agreed settlement, much like a mediator. In the end, though, trial is still a possibility.

Figure 4 is a table comparing leading dispute resolution methods against 10 factors that may be important in deciding which method is preferable in a particular dispute.

FIGURE 4 Comparison of Leading Dispute Resolution Methods Across 10 Factors.

Deciding Factors	Dispute Resolution Methods			
	Litigation	Arbitration	Mediation	Negotiation
1. Do costs make sense?	−	−	?	+
2. Are costs fixed or open/variable?	−	−	−	−
3. Reasonably fast process?	−	−	?	+
4. Does not require parties to agree?	+	−	−	−
5. Can a disappointed party appeal?	+	−	NA	NA
6. Is discovery robust *and* efficient?	−	−	?	−

Deciding Factors	Dispute Resolution Methods			
	Litigation	Arbitration	Mediation	Negotiation
7. Potential to save a relationship?	−	−	+	+
8. Sets precedent for any later disputes?	+	+	?	?
9. Stays private?	−	+	+	+
10. Is it fair?	+	+	+	?

Legend: " **+** " good, " **−** " bad, " **?** " depends on situation, " **NA** " not applicable

WE ARE HERE

Nonviolent dispute resolution is as old as human society. Early cultures adopted laws to govern human relations, leading to the establishment of courts and, eventually, to the promise of justice for all. Adversarial litigation driven by competing lawyers is a relatively recent phenomenon that has both important benefits and drawbacks. Because litigation is so costly, our society—and others before it—have sought to develop alternative dispute resolution methods. In the United States, arbitration and mediation have become the most popular of these. The former, however, has become so much like courtroom litigation that it has lost sight of its cost-cutting roots, and the latter, while sometimes very effective, is an unreliable solution that is subject to abuse.

Regardless of the ADR method used, it's apparent we've failed so far to create a more reliable, efficient, and effective dispute resolution answer for limited stakes disputes, because the focus has been on process, on rights, and on the benefits of having opposing advocates—and *not* on fast and fair resolution when litigation costs too much.

What's lacking is resolution-focused, stakes-sensitive justice. And so here we are.

CHAPTER SUMMARY

- Where we've been will always inform the way forward.

- China and Mesopotamia were the first human societies to codify laws. These initially focused on crimes, but the Code of Hammurabi specified situations and prescribed judgments that included common civil (noncriminal) disputes.

- The 12 Roman Tables and England's Magna Carta are foundations of modern U.S. law. The Romans (with Greek inspiration) introduced concepts like equal protection of laws for all citizens under a uniform written code, professional judges, right to legal representation, appeal, witness testimony subject to perjury, and punitive damages for some civil offenses. Magna Carta limited the powers of monarchs, introducing due process of law and trial by jury.

- The rise of lawyers as a profession was bumpy. The earliest "lawyers" had to be friends of parties and spoke without pay in Athenian court. Advertising for the privilege also was forbidden. The Romans encouraged client representation and turned that into a regulated profession, but the fall of Rome set lawyers back centuries, as the Germanic conquerors forbade them. Lawyers did not reemerge as an independent profession until the late Middle Ages, led by the English who strictly regulated their fees, roles, licensing, and—as witnessed by Shakespeare—appeared to hold them in generally low esteem.

- The American colonies expanded on Britain's approach to law and lawyers. The American Bar Association (ABA), formed in 1878 to help regulate the profession, accredits law schools and provides ethical guidelines, discipline, and continuing education.

- Legal fees in the U.S. initially were flat fees, capped by law, or subject to investigation by government authorities when excessive. They tended to be proportional to the value conferred. That changed in the late 1950s with a public relations campaign by the ABA and a switch by most lawyers to hourly based fees, except in contingency cases.

- In the U.S., the growth of uniform rules and due process has improved judicial fairness and transparency, but these improvements have also multiplied legal costs.

- ADR (Alternative Dispute Resolution) methods like arbitration and mediation have been used since ancient times as less formal, less expensive, more efficient paths to justice in many situations. Today, attorney advocacy too often makes them complex and costly. **Figure 4** compares leading dispute resolution methods across 10 factors.

"You have a pretty good case, Mr. Pitkin.
How much justice can you afford?"

CHAPTER 4

THE SCOPE OF THE PROBLEM

There's a core problem with our legal system: *It often serves lawyers much more than it does their clients.*

The number of lawyer jokes with analogies to sharks bears witness to the fact that we instinctively know this. In this chapter, we'll discuss three prime ways in which the system plainly promotes lawyers' interests over those of their clients to create a "perfect storm" of unintended and growing evil that is the plight of many common limited stakes disputes. These are:

- Hourly billing and the slow pace of litigation
- Our unbalanced obsession with due process
- The insane psychology of dispute resolution

Unfortunately, attempts to mitigate these attributes by addressing each separately have not worked. This chapter will demonstrate that what's required is an innovative, comprehensive solution that severely curtails their ability to impact real justice.

HOURLY BILLING AND THE SLOW PACE OF COURTROOM JUSTICE

Let's start by recognizing a fundamental reality—most plainly revealed in commercial disputes between trading or business partners: *We lawyers mostly charge by the hour. Not* by the project. *Not* by a portion of what is at stake. *Not* by the outcome.

If we didn't charge by the hour, we'd have every incentive to be frugal: Our financial interests would more closely align with those of our clients and our compensation would bear a closer and more reasonable relationship to the financial value we deliver. That would make a lot of sense to our clients. Of course, lawyers would face the risks of not being paid for work that we don't anticipate in advance, and of sharing responsibility for things we don't control—like our clients' misdeeds, truthfulness, and accuracy. That hardly seems fair. So we charge by the hour. The system serves us.

THERE'S NO RUSH

Not only do we lack incentive to be frugal with our clients' money but we also usually have little incentive or opportunity to get things done quickly. In fact, the system forces us to be deliberate and cautious. It's not just that we earn more fees by spending more time on tasks. No matter how efficient we may try to be, when we work behind closed doors and out of sight of our clients—for example, on research, analysis, brief-writing, or preparing witness examinations—we grapple with complicated issues and imprecise tactical, strategic, and human equations. It's not unlike a game of chess played on a three-dimensional platform: Sorting out all the factors and planning how best to present a client's position in the competition of a courtroom consume huge amounts of time, as do anticipating and responding to whatever the opposition may present. Then, when we work in the public eye and in the presence of clients, we're surrounded by an array of granular rules, conventions, processes, considerations, guidelines, risks, opposing attorneys, and neutral judges—such that anyone watching can see we have little control over the maddeningly slow pace of unfolding events.

Lawyers also are seldom at fault when opponents intentionally or irrationally slow everything down. Maneuver or mistake, it's all the same to us. While we may recognize the difference between the two, we know that our power to prevent the slowdown is near nonexistent.

So we're trained explicitly and implicitly that all this ritual and patience are necessary. Our professional legal duties of competence and zealous representation, as well as the specter of liability for malpractice, operate to slow our work and the pace of justice. We get used to it and acquiesce in it. We pride ourselves in our management of it. And it's certainly very good for our hourly based fees. In fact, *the slower the system works in the heat of battle, the better off we are.*

Finally, there's no Constitutional right to a speedy *noncriminal* trial. We may know in our minds and hearts that "justice delayed is justice denied," but not only is it *not* our responsibility, we don't see it in our power to fix.

Again, the system works for us.

Attorneys reading this may say, "Wait just a minute. We're constantly advising our clients to settle or simply forego claims and defenses that will cost more than they're worth, and clients who follow this advice avoid some or all of the delays and other costs of legal battles, including our fees." While this advice *can* be desirable and ethical behavior, it evades the core problem: Undue compromise or surrender of valid claims tends to leave people angry, frustrated, and without real justice.

OUR MYOPIC OBSESSION WITH DUE PROCESS

Unearthing truth is not our duty as lawyers. It's not our goal either. Our duty is to represent our client's best interests as effectively as possible within the constraints of the law. Our goal is to win, or at worst to minimize our client's loss. The theory behind adversarial process is that through zealous representation by capable counsel of competing parties' interests, truth will be revealed, and justice will be done.

BRIEF

While this book doesn't deal with criminal law, the best illustration of this concept is the criminal defense lawyer. A criminal defense lawyer's job is *not* to discover if the defendant is innocent or guilty and to bring that truth to the court, but to ensure that the defendant receives a zealous defense, and that the prosecution meets its constitutional burden to prove guilt beyond a reasonable doubt.

Of course, truth cannot be revealed and justice cannot be achieved without a relatively level playing field, so we have **rights**. Some rights are **substantive**, like the right of free speech, while others are **procedural**, like the right in civil cases to obtain the sworn testimony of a witness in a deposition before going to trial. Some are basic freedoms, while most are laws or regulations enacted for specific purposes. Most are intended to be the same for everyone, while some—usually legislated with a recognized public policy in mind—intentionally give some parties an advantage perceived as necessary to level the playing field in particular circumstances, such as statutes that authorize lawyers to put together class actions by many people having similar small claims against a large organization. All this is what we call **due process of law**.

Due process of law protects, but it also costs. The more protection, the more cost. It works kind of like insurance: How much is enough is usually unknown, so we lawyers—just like insurance salespeople—tend to advise that more is safer. In short, lawyers *love* due process—as much as we can get. It's what we're all about, and it puts food on the table. That's at least in part why we're forever advocating new and expanded rights and remedies, new laws, new regulations, new rules, new procedures—all in the name of due process.

Our allegiance to due process also naturally fosters in lawyers the belief that the best process is one that *lawyers* drive. We want to choose and control the tools, the strategies, the forum, and the witnesses—i.e., the show we'll put on (or at least threaten). Moreover, because we inherently want to see as much due process as possible, we want to maximize it not only in the courts but also in alternative processes like arbitration and mediation. Thus, whenever alternatives to court are introduced, lawyers want them to be lawyer-driven, with plenty of due process protections. Hence there's a tendency over time for alternatives like arbitration to increasingly look, feel, and cost like litigation, and for mediation to take place after at least some initial discovery and comprehensive briefing driven by dueling attorneys.

SIDEBAR

The Problem with Test Cases

It looked like I might get to argue before the United States Supreme Court.

We represented a reputable typewriter ribbon company who wanted to leverage its knowledge and expertise in ink to refill inkjet printer cartridges. This would save the company and reestablish its relevancy by helping businesses and consumers enjoy cheaper printing. The problem was that the computer and printer manufacturers definitely didn't like the idea. In fact, printer manufacturers designed and patented their cartridges like disposable razor blades to prevent anyone else from offering substitutes for them or reusing them—then they sued anyone who tried. We were litigating new, fascinating, and very important issues involving the intersection of intellectual property and antitrust laws, and the lower courts had been forced to rule on them without clear precedents as guidance.

As a lawyer, I was thrilled. For a litigator, arguing a case before the Supreme Court is the apex of lawyering. Our client, however, had mixed feelings. Appellate review, especially in the United States Supreme Court, devours time and money, and businesses small and large generally must pay their own legal fees in such explorations. Moreover, most business clients don't want to be a test case to set precedent or be part of a case that spends years going all the way to the Supreme Court. My client certainly did not. Businesses hate uncertainty, unpredictability, and delay. Moreover, they know that time and energy spent on helping the courts set publishable legal precedents are huge distractions from what businesses do best—irrespective of any long-term benefit to the cause of justice.

Some lawyers have argued that from a big-picture perspective, the costs for taking these precedent-setting cases to the highest courts are reasonable and it's our "duty" as citizens, including businesses, in a common law (precedent-based) justice system to suffer them. By this absurd logic, our legal system should forbid settlements in any disputes where novel legal issues may control or influence outcomes, because spending client and judicial resources in time and money and setting precedents for the future would always "serve the greater good." This is lawyer-centric thinking at its worst.

Businesses and individuals alike don't exist to serve our justice system, and they need to have the freedom to stop the bleeding when they choose. They're entitled to seek and expect a just process in their present circumstances, which should include an economically rational path to resolution of their dispute—rather than paying for some imagined and uncertain future dispute involving different parties, unknown stakes, and other circumstances. Where the stakes are high enough, they may rationally choose to endure the time and costs of adversarial trials, appeals, and other precedent-setting proceedings, but there is no justice in lining lawyers' pockets when stakes are moderate. Unfortunately, the incidence of the system serving lawyers more than clients is far more prevalent. In fact, in everyday disputes among commercial partners, it's the overwhelming rule rather than the exception.

In the case at hand—and fortunately for me—there was no choice. Without an applicable precedent, the only way to obtain justice for the client was to pursue the matter through the court hierarchy. In the end, I didn't get to stand in the hallowed halls of the Supreme Court and utter that famous opening line, "May it please the Court." Instead, the Supreme Court denied our petition without comment, as it often does. This meant that our client would need to go to trial with one hand tied behind its back, lose, and then appeal, before our side would get another real crack at justice. The law would later evolve in favor of our client, but not soon enough to save its business. Meanwhile, I got paid and lived to fight another day.

MORE PROCESS = MORE WORK = MORE COST

Due process ultimately requires that someone else—someone ideally neutral, reasonable, and intelligent—have the final authority to decide our clients' fate, so we must let ostensibly neutral judges, juries, and/ or arbitrators in the door. If we don't grant and trust in this authority, due process can become a kind of runaway anarchy that undermines essential freedoms and affordable justice alike.[1] Unfortunately, and in part because our heritage and culture are tied closely to the resistance of authority, our American judicial system and its popular alternatives take great care to relegate our neutral decision-makers to reactive, relatively passive roles as mere referees of our rights, while partisan lawyers drive all the action.

This is not the case in many foreign democratic nations having fair justice systems. In Germany, for example, judges play a proactive role early in the process—in investigating disputes and limiting discovery.[2] Consequently, considerations of reasonable proportion and economic rationality are embedded in every step of legal process there. By contrast, in the United States, judges and other neutral decision-makers are accustomed to and accept their more limited role. This saves them tedious work and allows them to focus on hearing and comparing the validity of competing stories with the intention—and authority—to decide what's true and just.

Maximum due process protections and lawyer-driven action arguably make sense in high stakes disputes, because by definition those stakes justify the corresponding high costs, whatever they might be. *These protections and roles, however, don't scale down well in limited stakes disputes.* For example, a dispute with only $50,000 at stake can hardly justify a lengthy process that enables and encourages battling attorneys on each side to employ $100,000 in time and fees in procedural sparring, document productions and review, witness interviews and depositions, motions, and hearings—not to mention the value of hidden costs like clients' distracted time, peace of mind, and damage to relationships and reputations.

Where is the justice in spending $100,000 (plus hidden costs) to get (or pay) $50,000? Shouldn't *real* justice cost some reasonable fraction of the stakes? *Yet the regular trial courts and their popular alternatives in America generally approach all disputes as "one size fits all" procedurally, and so their rules tend to deliver maximum protections in lawyer-driven process.*💡 In American courts, common limited stakes disputes—e.g., disputes with financial stakes in the range of $10,000 to $500,000—usually have the same essential set of due process protections and costs available in existential "bet-the-company," multimillion-dollar, and other perceived "must-win" situations.

BRIEF

The one major exception to this concept is small claims courts—where representation by attorneys is simply forbidden, usually in disputes with stakes less than $5,000 or $10,000 according to state law.

Some courts and private alternative dispute resolution forums have tried to account for this with pared down discovery rules, but with very limited impact. As state governments have found when setting up small claims courts, allocating different sets of rules for lower dollar value stakes without also eliminating lawyer-driven process is largely ineffective in bridging the injustice gap between small and high stakes disputes. Attorneys *will* find a way to circumvent efficiencies if we believe it's to a client's tactical or strategic advantage. The more procedural tools available to us, the more options we have and will use to that end. **Figure 5** illustrates the problematic relationship between more procedure and legal costs when stakes are limited.

FIGURE 5 Relationship of Procedure and Legal Costs When Stakes Are Limited.

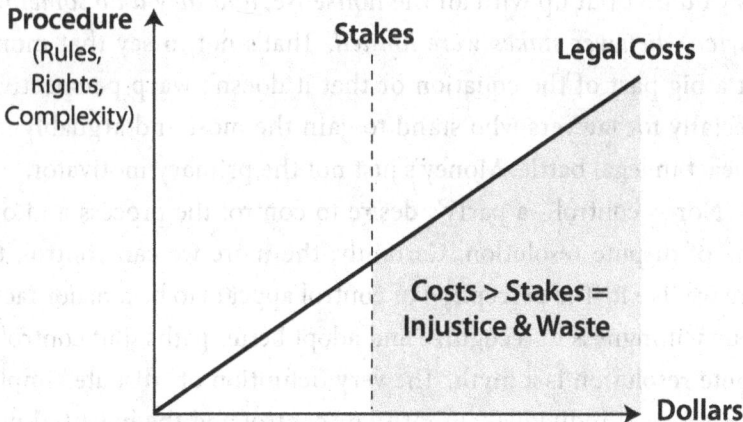

THE INSANE PSYCHOLOGY OF DISPUTES

I'm not a trained psychologist. However, I do have 42 years of professional experience dealing with unhappy people and their disagreements. I'm also a devoted student of the subject, reading scholarly works, articles, and case reviews, attending classes, and listening to lawyer "war stories." So, I ask you to at least be open to the following perspective about the psychology of dispute resolution as it applies here.

Human beings just can't help but get in their own way when it comes to dispute resolution. We so love playing the blame game that we sadly discount the costs and our own biases. Of course, the psychology of disputes is fascinating, and yes, I and countless other attorneys have built lucrative careers dealing with its realities. But from the perspective of advancing efficient justice, it's a huge obstacle.[3] Even good, smart people succumb to the special insanity that disagreements can trigger, while the foolish or greedy inevitably fall victim to opportunistic lawyers who count on that insanity and unfortunately give the rest of the legal profession a bad name.

What drives behavior in dispute resolution? What is the overarching psychological force? Surprisingly, it's *not* money. You don't need to be Warren Buffet to know that if it were just about money, clients wouldn't put up with all the nonsense, *and they'd do something smarter whenever stakes were limited.* That's not to say that money isn't a big part of the equation or that it doesn't warp perspectives, especially for lawyers who stand to gain the most and arguably risk the least in legal battle. Money's just not the primary motivator.

Nor is control—a party's desire to control the process and outcome of dispute resolution. Certainly, the more we can control, the more we like it. The perception of control appears to be a major factor in our willingness to recognize and adopt better paths. But control in dispute resolution is a myth. The very definition of "dispute" implies the absence of individual authority or control and the potential need for third-party intervention. The good news here, supported by scientifically sound empirical work, is that disputing parties by and large seem to understand and accept the need for neutral third-party control of both process and outcome.[4]

Not surprisingly, disputing parties have preferences for the terms on which they will cede ostensible control: They want assurances of a fair process (including the clear opportunity to tell their story and know it's been heard), a skilled and neutral decision-maker, and, for most people, transparency and direct participation.[5] To the extent that an attorney can help deliver those assurances, people want legal representation, but having a lawyer present their case doesn't seem to be a condition to surrendering control.[6] In fact, most people would prefer to present their own case to a third party rather than have their lawyer do so in their absence.[7] In sum, people generally are willing to give up control when just a few reasonable, principled conditions are met, and particularly if doing so will save them money and time, *unless* their attorney, whose advice they likely will follow, guides them differently.[8]

So, if neither money nor control is the primary driver of behavior in dispute resolution, what is?

The number one driver of behavior in dispute resolution—drumroll please—is our desire for *vindication*, or, in other words, our quest to right a perceived wrong against us. Even in situations where the brain's instinctive first reaction is to flee instead of fight, circumstances usually compel us to fight—to resist the wrong being done us—at least to some degree.[9] Put less admirably, this primary driver of our actions is a form of getting even, exacting revenge, or laying blame elsewhere. Sometimes it even includes inflicting pain or punishment, or making an opponent pay for or stop doing something that we believe is wrong.

Considering that love and self-preservation are among the most powerful motivators of human behavior, it shouldn't be a surprise that a self-righteously propelled fervor for vindication or vengeance follows closely behind. We *hate* perceived injustice with our whole being—not just our pride and egos. Especially when we are the victims, we hate injustice *so much* that it hurts and we must do something about it, whether we're accuser or accused.

The desire for vengeance is also one of the most *blinding* motivators of our behavior. When we feel that sense of wrongness inflicted by someone or something outside of ourselves, we lose our emotional balance and can't see straight. No less an authority than the Holy Bible recognizes this truth and admonishes us to reserve vengeance to God. Unfortunately, that lofty but impractical solution runs contrary to human nature and real-world circumstance, so we don't just turn the other cheek lest we allow evil to run amok. Instead, we go to war.

In response to these realities, civilized society has evolved the concept of **justice**, with courts to administer it. In the adversarial system of justice popular today, we lawyers play the role of warrior champions—usually without the blood. And that's a very good and worthy thing. Unfortunately, adversarial process doesn't effectively right wrongs in most common, limited stakes conflicts. In fact, it exacerbates them, not just monetarily, but also psychologically.

FANNING FLAMES

As I write this, parts of my home state, California, are ablaze in uncontrolled brush and forest fires. High winds fan the flames of those fires, causing them to spread and multiplying the damage. Imagine for a moment these fires are common wrongs needing to be stopped, while the winds represent lawyer-driven legal battles. You begin to feel the heat of the problem.

Please note that I'm talking here only about lawyers' roles in *formal legal process*. There's no substitute for the help a good lawyer can be from the moment he or she is asked to assess a client's rights and prospects for success or to negotiate a settlement, right up until or even beyond the point that formal legal action starts. Of course, an opportunistic or careless lawyer can easily stoke the flames of a client's sense of injustice or an opponent's competitive drive in ways that lead away from imminent containment, but that occurs less frequently than you might suspect.

While the problem *can be* lawyers agitating by choice, even those of us who don't so intend can unwittingly fan the flames of irrational conflict. The reasons are legion, and nonlawyers need to understand them to escape getting burned over and over again.

First, lawyers wrongly believe we can control the future course and costs of a contest, so we *routinely* underestimate both the time and costs that will be expended, which effectively encourages our clients to fight longer. In 42 years of practice, I've seldom seen lawyers' pre-litigation *projections* of total legal fees and related costs approach or exceed the *actual* costs later incurred. Instead, our projections are *low* because we either omit tasks by mistake, miscalculate actual "all-in" times to complete tasks, or underestimate the irrationality around us. Moreover, we almost never include estimates of hidden and difficult-to-value client costs, such as distracted productive time, undue stress, and the risks of lost reputations or relationships.

> *Lawyers wrongly believe we can control the future course and costs of a contest, so we routinely underestimate both the time and costs that will be expended, which effectively encourages our clients to fight longer.*

Second, we tend to overestimate our clients' chances of success because we don't use disciplined probability analysis to account for everything we should. Moreover, we and our clients naturally prefer an optimistic and positive prognosis, and clients often don't know or omit harmful facts which later will prove important. In any event, good probability analysis takes time and focus, including identifying all realistically possible final outcomes and the principal events that *must* come to pass for each outcome to occur, then assigning probabilities to each outcome or event. When the separate probabilities are multiplied, what may have appeared upon first impression to have an enticing 80% likelihood of success is far more likely to have a significantly lower actual probability. Consequently, few lawyers even engage in this task.

Third, we *want* to believe our clients, so we're suckers for a sympathetic story and persevere longer than good sense would allow. This is a form of **confirmation bias**, also sometimes aptly, if colloquially, named **myside** bias. It's the cognitive tendency to search for, interpret, favor, and recall information in a way that confirms one's preexisting beliefs or wants, while ignoring or unfairly discounting alternatives. In human relations, it drives us to associate with like-minded people, and it's one of the great obstacles to reasoned discourse and mutual respect, a primary cause of intolerance, and a bane of peaceful coexistence. Confirmation bias is always the path of least resistance and the enemy of any balanced examination of issues on which reasonable people may disagree. It naturally pulls lawyers and clients alike into its jaws like a hungry crocodile.

Fourth, we always *do believe* that we can help, and we want to do so. If a client's goals include inflicting pain or punishment on an opponent, or making that opponent pay or stop doing something, we have the legal knowledge, tools, weapons, and (perhaps unfortunately) the incentive to try to deliver that outcome.

Fifth, if there's a lawyer on the other side, we believe the client needs us. We're usually right about this where adversarial process is concerned. A litigant *without* a lawyer who faces a litigant *with* one is indeed at a severe disadvantage in a forum where knowing and following correct procedure can be the margin of victory or defeat.

Last but by no means least, we unwittingly fan flames of irrational conflict because lawyers are as human as our clients. We're similarly susceptible to emotionally triggered fight responses due to insult, abuse, challenge, or other provocation by opposing counsel—which inevitably leads to retaliation and near-nuclear proliferation.

A LARGE AND GROWING INJUSTICE GAP

It's reasonable to ask, "So what if our legal system better serves lawyers than it does justice in some limited range of disputes? Lawyers need to eat too, right?" You might also wonder if this isn't actually a problem, but merely the natural and inevitable price of having the best legal system in the world. Since most nonlawyers have only rare direct experience with the justice system, the impact could be negligible. What proof is there that this is even a real crisis worth addressing?

Unfortunately, there's no comprehensive reported data on the size and scope of the gap in civil justice described in this book: There's no data on the percentage of cases in which each side's legal fees have consumed most or all of what was at stake and by how much. There's no data on how many additional cases lawyers turn down each year because they know they can't deliver economically rational service in light of what is or isn't at stake. There's no data on the frequency with which businesses and individuals choose to forego justice by deciding not to bring or oppose legal claims because they perceive that legal and other costs—what I call the *total costs of litigation*—will exceed the time, money, and trouble that getting justice is worth. *And there are no obligations or incentives in our adversarial justice system to seek or report these percentages, numbers, or frequency.*

BRIEF

Despite the lack of hard data, it *is* possible to create a useful model and calculator for **total costs of litigation**—at least in any given limited stakes dispute. An online version of such a calculator is free and readily available to anyone wishing to use it at https://www.justresolve.com/tcl-calculator/.

Nevertheless, there's no question that the civil injustice gap is a huge and growing problem. After speaking about this with hundreds of lawyers, *all* have readily acknowledged it and most have faced it frequently in their careers—usually in the context of negotiating, litigating, discouraging, or declining cases which they knew or suspected would cost more than what was at stake. The proof, however, is far more than anecdotal. There are countless articles, studies, and data sources from a wide range of perspectives that either explicitly or indirectly recognize this problem:

- Only 4% of civil cases filed in state court go to trial. "Litigation costs that routinely exceed the case value explain the low rate of dispositions involving any form of formal adjudication."[10]

- The discovery and trial phases of a lawsuit encompass 53% to 75% of total attorney hours incurred in common legal disputes that go to trial. Focus on these phases is imperative to successful judicial reform.[11]

- In 2015, the American Arbitration Association reported filings of $16 billion in claims and counterclaims in 8,360 business-to-business (B2B) commercial cases alone, most of which involved stakes less than $500,000 per case.[12]

- A 2012 survey of attorneys estimated that median legal costs in state court contract cases through the trial phase were $91,000. Ten years earlier, the median judgment in such cases was only $70,000. Even adjusting for inflation, this suggests that legal costs in fact exceed stakes in common B2B and other contract cases.[13]

- A conservative extrapolation of the overall size of the injustice gap problem in civil, non-small claims commercial and contract lawsuits with stakes below $500,000 suggests that there are over 250,000 such disputes annually with corresponding legal costs of over $23 billion.[14] Since an estimated six million civil cases are filed each year in the United States and the injustice gap is not limited to common commercial and contract disputes, the problem may be significantly larger than the extrapolation suggests.[15]

- Since at least the mid-1980s, the United States Department of Justice (DOJ) and legal commentators and professionals have known and been concerned about the high costs of what was then called "ordinary" civil litigation. At that time, the DOJ funded a broad study of the subject, called *The Civil Litigation Research Project* (CLRP) based primarily on court case files and lengthy postmortem interviews of the litigating attorneys. Using terms like **modest, ordinary, everyday, typical**, and **middle range** to describe its focus on limited stakes cases, and **rare** and **extraordinary** to distinguish high stakes cases, the project's three-volume report and follow-on publications examined stakes and the "gap" phenomenon to shed light on the costs of civil justice. Unfortunately, its reliance on attorney interviews and a high percentage of cases settled before trial prevented a full accounting of costs of litigation.[16]

- Over 90% of all non-small claims commercial disputes arising in our judicial system have stakes below $500,000, while well less than 10% make up the higher stakes, i.e., extraordinary large and complex cases that tend to be broadly reported in the news media.[17]

- A 2017 study of how delayed justice impacts business, commissioned by the American Arbitration Association, found that for legal disputes with $75,000 or more at stake, courts typically take at least twice as long as arbitrations through trial or award. The economic costs of this delay (*regardless of outcome and without including the huge role of legal fees*) more than *double* the costs of getting to resolution—adding at least $28.3 to $35.3 billion annually nationwide in the segment of the legal market studied. Justice delayed is truly justice denied.[18]

- In the only other study found that has tried to quantify some of the hidden costs of litigation, the costs of lost and distracted time were estimated to add 25% to total costs incurred.[19]

By any measure, whether one's perspective is big picture or uniquely personal, both the scope of this problem and the need for real solutions are great.

SIDEBAR

Elusive Stats

It's not easy to reliably estimate the size of the limited stakes justice gap. Efforts to study magnitudes and trends in civil litigation by the National Center for State Courts (NCSC), Federal Court Management Statistics (FCMS), and others simply don't break down data based on financial stakes. Moreover, they can't account for the huge impact of private and unreported arbitrations, mediations, settlement negotiations, and business decisions to forego claims and defenses based on anticipated excessive costs of litigation. Also, the data available on dispute numbers and legal fees expended varies tremendously. For example, recent estimates of the entire national legal services market vary by a factor of four, from $100 billion to $427 billion.[20]

The NCSC, however, has expressly acknowledged the justice gap: "For most represented litigants, the costs of litigating a case through trial would greatly exceed the monetary value of the case. In some instances, the costs of even initiating the lawsuit or making an appearance as a defendant would exceed the value of the case . . ."[21]

Law firms and lawyers don't report aggregated data on stakes, outcomes, or net client financial value delivered by dispute type, or other useful segmentation (e.g., contract/business disputes below $500,000 stakes). It's simply not in their training or interest to do so. Other complicating factors include differences in billing rates and realization based on kind of service (e.g., litigation vs. transactional), the far greater numbers of disputes with far lower stakes that fall into the gap, the absence of insurance coverage for most of these disputes, and the overriding fact that the size of the dispute depends on the eye of the beholder. While the low end of the gap tends to correspond to the upper limit of small claims court (typically $10,000 or less), attorneys and company executives give widely different answers as to the upper end, ranging between $99,000 and $2,000,000. My own crude extrapolations use a range of $10,000 to $500,000.

CHAPTER SUMMARY

- The limited stakes problem described earlier causes an immense and ever-growing **civil injustice gap** in America.

- When stakes are limited, our civil justice system serves lawyers more effectively than it does their clients. This manifests in at least three primary ways:

  — The hourly billing tradition and slow pace of justice

  — Our obsession with due process

  — The psychology of dispute resolution

- The practice of hourly billing creates little financial incentive for lawyers to be frugal or to get things done quickly. This favors lawyer interests over clients.

- Our adversarial justice system works slowly, regardless of who is at fault, which favors lawyer interests over clients.

- Due process of law protects, but at a cost. The more protection, the more cost. Lawyers tend to advocate for more due process, and it puts food on the table.

- Most courts and their alternatives have essentially "one size fits all" sets of procedural rules for cases above small claims court jurisdiction. That has some efficiencies, but not for delivering real justice with costs proportional to stakes. Experiments with pared-down procedures tend to make little difference because the underlying process is still lawyer-driven.

- The psychology of disputes serves lawyers by tending to promote conflict. The natural desire for vindication or vengeance causes clients to seek what they believe is justice, while lawyers tend to underestimate the likely and total costs of litigation, overestimate the chances of "winning," succumb to convenient confirmation bias, and are susceptible to being provoked to anger and retaliation by adversaries.

- Available data confirms the existence, substantial magnitude, and growth of the civil injustice gap, despite years of lip service condemning it and sporadic efforts to control it.

Cartoon Resource/
Shutterstock.com

"I'm sure there's an escape clause somewhere."

CHAPTER 5

TOWARDS A SOLUTION THAT WORKS

So there I was. The year was 2005. My legal experience, my farm up-bringing, and my business CEO group were all preaching a single message: In most everyday civil cases, the judicial system costs so much that it is effectively broken.

When I couldn't settle these cases early enough—and that happened too often given limited knowledge, high distrust, big ego, or avarice on at least one side—I knew that I likely wouldn't be able to deliver real justice to my clients. Justice would either take too long and cost too much, or else the clients would have to walk away from their rights at some point—either giving up a good claim or succumbing to extortion.

I found this deeply troubling. Worse, too many of my opponents—lawyers and businesspeople alike—and even some of my own clients, were so "win-focused," emotionally triggered, culturally brainwashed, or just plain greedy, that they would persevere deep into the litigation process, or even through to its end, rather than—rather than—what?

Really, what *was* my clients' alternative to this Hobson's Choice of disappointing and unjust paths? So many would-be solutions had been tried and found wanting. How would one go about finding or creating a real solution? And, if a good solution could be identified, who would champion it? It wouldn't be the large law firm lawyers, whose big and complex cases justify and can afford their services (and deliver their livelihoods), nor other lawyers who fear loss of control and fees, nor the traditional ADR services who make money marketing arbitration and traditional mediation to lawyers, nor the people and businesses who simply want to "win" at all costs.

BRIEF

"Hobson's Choice" is a **choice to take what is offered or nothing at all**—to "take it or leave it." The expression comes from the mid-17th century and was named after Thomas Hobson, a Cambridge livery stable owner/operator who hired out horses by giving the customer the choice of the one nearest the door or none at all.

With all the resistance that likely would come from these entrenched interests, I asked myself why I should even consider taking this on. With what arrogance dare I think that *I* might come up with a real answer that no one else had in over 200 years? What are all the reasons that it could and probably would fail? What would such an uncertain endeavor cost? And why challenge a system that had handsomely fed and clothed me for twenty-six years? In short, what the *hell* was I thinking?

I was thinking that people deserve justice. I was thinking, as do the lawyers I most respect, that my clients—individuals, businesses, and other organizations alike—all should be able to get justice without undue cost, waste, stress, and distraction from what they do best. I was thinking that a lot of good people are sued or forced to sue every year, paying exhorbitant costs in hard-earned money to a greedy and inefficient justice system. I also was thinking that maybe I was in a uniquely opportune position and stage in my career and life, and had broad enough experience and perspective to see what was wrong and possibly do something about it. And I thought that just maybe our culture has arrived at the right time and place to accept needed change.

In short, I was thinking I might be able to make a difference for good, and that I had enough passion and resources to try. At a minimum, a life-learning adventure lay ahead.

DON'T THROW OUT THE BABY
WITH THE BATHWATER

So I dug in. First, I tried to identify what a real solution would look and feel like, including which elements of our current system needed to stay, and which needed to go.

Our forefathers believed (as does virtually every litigator in America, excluding a cynical minority) that our traditional adversarial process and its procedural protections, in combination, afford the greatest opportunity for both achieving and evolving quality, reliable justice over time. As a former career litigator, I confess that in high stakes disputes I still believe this to be true.

One need only look at what passes for or purports to be justice in autocratic societies to see the overall merit to our system. Consequently, in the context of identifying and nurturing a solution for the gap in justice in limited stakes disputes in America, it behooves any would-be solution to retain those elements of our adversarial system that are critical to, and make the most impact on, achieving a reliably comparable, high quality of justice.

On the other hand, I also recognized that a real solution would need to depart greatly from the status quo in ways that both substantially *reduce* several types of costs inherent in traditional legal process and *overcome* each of the cultural and psychological influences that drive and reinforce that process.

Through experience, research, and interviews, the critical elements of a real solution emerged fairly quickly:

- **A truly fair and transparent process.** This includes high integrity, competency, transparency, a level playing field in investigation and decision-making that is blind to wealth and influence, and an all-important mutual "say" in who is selected to execute those roles.

- **A mutually agreed and expert judge.** Both efficiency and "buy in" to any process greatly improve when parties have a say in who will decide their fate and that person has experience with the industry, field, or other key subject matter of the disagreement.

- **Full opportunity for each side to tell their story.** 💡 Sometimes called "voice" or the right to one's day in court, both logic and published studies recognize the *opportunity to be heard* as one of the most critical elements for achieving justice and, perhaps just as important, enabling confidence in and acceptance (however begrudging) of the fairness of any resolution process and its outcome. This element includes the opportunities to communicate one's wants or goals and to identify what information is believed important and worth considering.

BRIEF

The opportunity for each side to tell their story helps explain the challenge that online dispute resolution processes have in gaining acceptance and reliably delivering justice. This and similar features are sometimes collectively referred to as the "human" element in dispute resolution—something at which inflexible formulaic classifications and computer algorithms don't yet excel.

- **Resolution in weeks instead of years.** When stakes are limited, slow justice means no justice. Lengthy process and delay unduly rob us of precious time, focus, energy, money, and peace of mind, while rewarding only maneuver, suspicion, and cynicism. Even the best-intentioned lawyers cannot control the huge time-and-cost-multiplying impacts of repeatedly needing to coordinate and accommodate multiple schedules and deal with the inevitable delays—both natural and artificial—that occur in the course of adversarial due process.

- **A robust and reliable investigation.** The process should enable identifying and gathering from all parties the pertinent records, witness testimony, and other information necessary to learn the truth and resolve the dispute correctly. When needed, this should include the opportunity to ask witnesses hard questions, and judicial-like authority to enforce compliance and deter or punish any failure to cooperate or disclose requested information—for example, by drawing adverse inferences about key facts when related records have been destroyed or tampered with. A robust and reliable investigation creates a high likelihood of unearthing truth, reaching a just result, and gaining the parties' confidence in a process and result. It is an especially powerful and necessary counterbalance against susceptibility to errors, lying, and efforts to hide important information.

- **The right to have legal counsel, and if necessary, a spokesperson.** There are many legitimate reasons why some people want or need this, even if they're perfectly willing to grant a neutral third party the authority to investigate and decide their dispute in a manner that limits what their legal counsel can demand or do.

- **A cooperative, non-adversarial search for truth.** This is the only way to jettison the big ticket costs of litigation that don't make economic sense. These costs include formal discovery procedures, formal briefing and motion cycles, trial preparation, formal trial or hearings, scheduling coordination and complexities, redundant research, multiple "hired gun" experts, and other opportunities for inflaming greed, resentment, and suspicion via gamesmanship, maneuver, burden, delay, and other tools of psychological warfare. In short, the process needs to eliminate or severely curtail the standard tools of litigation advocacy that are typically available to opposing parties and their attorneys who seek to "win" at all costs or gain undue advantage.

- **Decisions, with analysis, that invite comment or challenge before becoming final, and allow a right of review to minimize risk of bias.** One of the great strengths—however costly—of our judicial system is its multiple opportunities for review of possibly mistaken or biased rulings, verdicts, and judgments. Decision-makers are humans, and humans make mistakes or can be subverted—consciously or subconsciously—by improper interests. It's therefore important in a trustworthy alternative process to create efficient opportunities to correct wrong decisions without unduly multiplying time and cost. Where this can be done, it will enhance the reliability and credibility of the process. For example, since most wrong decisions are caused by honest mistakes, requiring a draft final decision that is tentative and invites question, challenge, or comment, would cause minimal cost and delay while serving justice well.💡 However, since a tentative decision loop *may not* cure a huge blind spot and *won't* cure an unforeseen, highly biased result, there ought to be a practical right of expedited appeal, at least where the aggrieved party is willing to pay for it. (On the other hand, this may not be necessary in a dispute where the risk of such bias already has been tempered by using multiple decision-makers, such as a three-person neutral tribunal).

BRIEF

Many courtroom judges throughout the United States routinely use such **tentative rulings** and similar mechanisms in most important procedural orders and final decisions.

- **A truly affordable process.** *Affordable* here means two things: First, that the total costs of seeking and obtaining justice (mostly legal fees and related costs) should make economic sense, and therefore not exceed some reasonable and proportional fraction of the value—usually the amount of money—that is realistically at stake in the dispute. In short, total costs *should not* approach, equal, or exceed financial stakes. Second, "affordable" also means that those same total costs in absolute terms are low enough to be within the reach of all sides.

- **Minimal hidden costs.** Hidden costs must be severely curtailed. These costs, as defined earlier, encompass the value of distracted productive time of the parties in a dispute resolution process, and also the parties' unnecessary stress, reduced cash flow, and risks of incidental loss of reputation or otherwise salvageable relationships.

- **Fixed or capped professional fees and other out-of-pocket costs.** Eliminating open-ended legal costs reduces conflicts of interest (such as an hourly paid lawyer's inherent incentive not to settle early) and aligns important interests among all involved. It also enables much better informed decisions at the outset, reduces overall costs, and permits effective resource planning and cash management.

- **Flexibility.** Different kinds of disputes may warrant different steps, rules, or tools. Some disputes may benefit from mediation, assured privacy and confidentiality, special agreement on who will pay fees and costs, or even an expert's or jury's take on a critical issue. A good process is one that can adapt to special needs and not pretend that one size or shape fits all.

- **A binding outcome whenever possible, with high costs for noncompliance and noncooperation.** Nonbinding processes often fail, increasing costs of every kind without meaningfully improving the likelihood of a better net outcome. A court-enforceable final decision with strong disincentives for noncompliance and process rules that deter noncooperation are necessary to give *any* resolution process the teeth it needs to succeed for all parties. Having a principled decision as the endgame of the process (barring a mutually acceptable settlement) also satisfies the all-important psychological drive to right a wrong, at least for the party who wins on the merits.

- **Savings and benefits so great, apparent, demonstrable, and readily available that they overcome both cultural and psychological barriers to change, as well as the entrenched interests and inertia that perpetuate those barriers.** This element of the solution could be the most difficult to achieve. It requires assembling a compelling case and creating an effective education and awareness effort by credible and well-meaning people targeting businesses, government, individuals, law schools, lawyers and other legal professionals. Such a campaign must anticipate and combat likely disinformation and FUD (fear, uncertainty and doubt) from entrenched interests. Finally, some neutral administrative services and reputable neutral professionals need to step forward to include and promote the new process in their offerings.

Insofar as most of the above elements come from or compare with practices in American courtrooms, **Figure 6** attempts to list and compare them for assessing which to keep or discard in crafting a reliable yet economically practical resolution method for limited stakes disputes.

FIGURE 6 What to Keep and What to Toss.

KEEP	TOSS
☑ Fair and Transparent Process	☒ Unfair Advantages and Secrecy
☑ Mutually Agreed Expert Judge	☒ Assigned Judge
☑ Personal Voice/Opportunity to Be Heard	☒ Unneeded or Inflamed Confrontations
☑ Assured Short Duration	☒ Ability to Stall and Delay
☑ Robust, Truth-Focused Investigation	☒ Formal Competitive Discovery
☑ Advice of Counsel	☒ Counsel-Driven Advocacy
☑ Correctable Binding Decisions	☒ Expensive Appeals
☑ Fixed Costs Proportionate to Stakes	☒ Open-Ended Costs That Consume Stakes
☑ Simple and Flexible Procedure	☒ Complex and Rigid Procedure
☑ Incentives to Cooperate	☒ Incentives to Compete

THE SOLUTION: NEUTRAL-DRIVEN PROCESS

Satisfied with the elements identified above, I proceeded to study the largest costs in legal disputes—legal bills—and ran different conceptual scenarios for dispute resolution processes. This led me to revisit, in a manner of speaking, Shakespeare's earlier-cited solution from *Henry VI* to "kill all the lawyers."[1] More forgiving, my scenarios confirmed that the *only* way to solve the limited stakes justice problem is to severely curtail the process-driving role and prerogatives that competing lawyers have in these disputes. That doesn't mean we need to eliminate them entirely—nor should we. We just need to rein them in.

As trusted advisors, informed lawyers are the first line of defense against injustice. They know the field far better than their clients. They can advise and often protect against unnecessary and unduly expensive or stressful paths. They may be able to resolve a conflict early through negotiation. They are the loyal strategists and capable warriors who fight for clients' rights when needed. In short, they have invaluable, critical roles to play in almost all legal disputes.

In some relationships and disputes, however, we now know that if we let our lawyers carry our dispute past early negotiation efforts and down the traditional path of legal pleading, formal discovery, procedural maneuvering, prolific brief-writing, and trial (or trial-like) advocacy, it is almost certain that they will cost us far more than they are worth— that is, far more than the difference their advocacy is likely to make.

We understand this, at least intellectually. But what's the *alternative* in these no-win scenarios? We may be tempted to think that this hole, or gap, in justice is a small price we must pay to get justice the rest of the time. But wait. These no-win scenarios *are* the rest of the time. They *are* the lion's share of disputes that real people face, regardless of frequency. In the words of legendary radio broadcaster Paul Harvey, they *are* "the rest of the story"[2] that makes their solution the real takeaway here.

The answer, like most truly better ideas, is so simple that we're reluctant to believe it works. The answer *must be* and is a *neutral-driven resolution ("NDR")* process, where the neutrals who will ultimately decide the dispute are the same persons who proactively oversee and conduct the dispute's investigation and legal analysis. As a direct consequence, in NDR *all effort that used to be undertaken and controlled by opposing lawyers in order to seek advantage for their clients is focused instead on seeking truth and applying applicable legal principles in order to deliver a just result.* This allows the parties to continue to both strongly disagree with each other and to seek principled vindication, while the process itself becomes *non-adversarial* and *collaborative* through its control by one or more investigating neutral judges. *As we will see, the potential savings in legal and hidden costs from this singular process innovation are both profound and inevitable.*

SIDEBAR

In the future, not all judges may be human. Advances in **online dispute resolution (ODR)** will lead to decision-making methods that are guided by artificial intelligence. As with current developments in self-driving cars, we are coming to recognize and accept that computers can help us make better decisions on the road. This same development is now foreseeable in dispute resolution. Of course, the Baby Boomer skeptic in me still believes that the psychology and other dynamics and nuances of dispute resolution will require human adjudicatory intervention for decades to come. Whether or not the decision-making is human, neutral-driven process and ODR have similar goals and should be very compatible.

CHAPTER SUMMARY

- If we believe that people and organizations deserve justice, then something needs to be done to solve the limited stakes problem and resulting justice gap.

- It makes sense that any real solution needs to keep those elements of our adversarial system that are critical to achieving a reliably high quality of justice.

- On the other hand, that same solution also must leave behind practices that perpetuate the kinds of absurd costs that typically consume limited stakes, and the cultural and psychological barriers that trigger behaviors which prevent real justice.

- My investigation revealed that a real solution therefore should deliver *all* of the following: a fair and transparent process, an agreed judge with subject matter expertise, full opportunity for each side to tell their story, fast resolution in weeks rather than years, robust and cooperative investigation of factual truth and applicable law, right to confidential advice and a spokesperson if necessary, written and explained decisions with an opportunity to question or challenge, total costs that are fixed (or capped) and proportional to stakes, adaptability to different circumstances, a binding outcome whenever possible with adequate penalties to deter noncompliance or noncooperation, and large enough net savings and benefits to overcome cultural and psychological resistance to adoption.

- The solution is a **Neutral-Driven Resolution ("NDR")** process that severely curtails the roles and prerogatives of dueling lawyers.

- In NDR, the person(s) who will ultimately decide the dispute are also the persons who proactively conduct and control its investigation in a neutral, non-adversarial, and collaborative way.

- In NDR, *almost all effort is focused on seeking truth rather than "winning" or other competitive advantage.* This accommodates strong disagreement and the opportunity to seek vindication while assuring an economically rational process and better net result for *all* sides in limited stakes disputes. In other words, NDR can deliver real justice.

"We would like to request a change of venue to an entirely different legal system."

CHAPTER 6

NDR: A SIMPLE PROCESS

The really good news is that Neutral-Driven Resolution (NDR) is not rocket science. Like open-source software, it's available to all for the asking, isn't secret, and is not "owned" by anyone. It consists of three simple, basic steps.

STEP ONE: CHOOSE

All parties must *choose* by written agreement to use NDR for their dispute. This includes a set of fair rules and principles to follow and one or more *agreed* and willing neutral judges or experts (Neutrals) to lead the process and ultimately decide the parties' differences.💡 The Neutrals must be vetted and qualified for potential conflicts of interest (just like courtroom judges), for appropriate subject matter expertise, and for appropriate resolution skills, then either be approved by all parties or chosen by process of elimination from a panel of qualified candidates.

BRIEF

In legal terms, the process and written agreement should be court enforceable in order to protect the prevailing party against potential noncompliance by the disappointed party.

The realities of civil litigation discussed in Chapter 4 make this first step the hardest, and it's much easier to describe than to achieve. Choosing to act logically and intelligently is easy to conceptualize and accept in principle, but is fraught with mini-devils in the details. Fortunately, there's more good news at this point: Help is available in making these choices—even in persuading uninformed or reluctant parties to join—which we'll discuss later.

The choice to use NDR is much more easily made *before* there's a dispute. Where parties know each other and already have an existing business or personal relationship, NDR can be briefly specified in whatever written business or other contract they may make together at a time when optimism and trust tend to be high. (The parties need not select Neutrals nor determine other administrative details unless a dispute arises—as is common practice in arbitration and mediation pre-dispute contract clauses as well.) If that's not possible—if there *is* no relationship or no prior agreement to resolve future disputes in this manner—the choice can be made in a fully detailed contract between the disputants *when their differences arise.* This is much harder, of course, because now at least one of the parties is probably disappointed or angry with the other, and both are likely to be suspicious of *anything* that the other thinks is a good idea.

In my preferred version of NDR, the parties use an independent, high-integrity *neutral coordinating service* to oversee and facilitate the process, including setting rules and vetting neutral candidates. Also, when the parties agree to the Neutrals, they and the Neutrals agree to a *fixed or not-to-exceed fee* to be paid for the whole process—a fee that is a proportional fraction of the apparent financial stakes involved and reflects other basic preliminary information about the nature of the dispute and what resources should be needed to resolve it correctly.

A fixed or capped fee is a critical element because any process that relies on open-ended, hourly fee billing by the Neutrals could prove almost as disastrous as the attorney-driven process it replaces. Fortunately, NDR Neutrals are comfortable quoting and committing to a reasonable fixed or capped fee in advance, because the amount and nature of the work that they will need to do is definable and controllable within an acceptable, reasonable margin of error. Finally, each party can designate who will speak for them, although in neutral-driven process the opportunities and need for lawyer *argument* and other forms of *advocacy* are extremely limited and subject to the broad discretion of the Neutrals. See **Appendix B** for a model complete written agreement with rules.💡

💡 BRIEF

The sample agreement and rules in **Appendix B** refer to NDR Neutrals as "Arbiters" and to the NDR process itself as a "resolve." These are preferred terms used in my NDR service. I don't use them in the main text here in order to avoid possible confusion, such as between "Arbiter" and "Arbitrator," or in use of the word "resolve."

STEP TWO: INVESTIGATE

The Neutrals in NDR then actively investigate the pertinent facts and law with broad discretion, as well as a focus on finding truth and fairly deciding the dispute. More specifically, the Neutrals *personally* interview the parties about what happened, what they know, what they want, and what they think is important. They also request and obtain pertinent records and other evidence, including interviews with other key witnesses. This investigation into facts and law essentially tracks one of the primary roles that attorneys typically play in a lawsuit, except that this investigation's focus is entirely on efficient *truth-seeking* for the benefit of all, rather than *advantage-seeking* for the benefit of a single client. If a party is discovered to be untruthful or fails to cooperate fully and promptly, the Neutrals may use this against the offender when deciding the dispute. If confidentiality of certain information is important, the Neutrals can take appropriate steps to preserve it. The Neutrals also research applicable legal and equitable principles as warranted.

> *This investigation into facts and law essentially tracks one of the primary roles that attorneys typically play in a lawsuit, except that this investigation's focus is entirely on efficient* **truth-seeking** *for the benefit of all, rather than* **advantage-seeking** *for the benefit of a single client.*

STEP THREE: RESOLVE

Finally, the Neutrals analyze and evaluate the facts in light of the law and decide the dispute in a fully explained writing. The parties must promptly and fully comply with the decision or face enforcement in court. A noncomplying party should be obligated to pay all fees and costs of both the process just completed and any necessary judicial enforcement.

In my preferred version, the Neutrals issue a preliminary or provisional decision and invite the parties to react and comment in order to minimize the risk of having overlooked or misunderstood something important to the analysis. This "tentative ruling" loop also minimizes the risks to a party of feeling blind-sided, helpless, and unheard by a surprise line of thought or finding. After reviewing the parties' feedback, the Neutrals have discretion to amend or adopt the provisional decision and make it final, or even briefly to reopen the investigation as appropriate.

FLEXIBILITY—TWO OPTIONAL STEPS

If the parties are so inclined, there are two optional steps, either or both of which can be readily included in an NDR process.

One is an **expedited mediation** step. This simply authorizes the Neutrals to facilitate mutually desired settlement negotiations at some point during the investigation step, preferably *after* reasonable investigation. In this mediation, the Neutrals should have full discretion about how to conduct the talks. The mediation step adds flexibility at little or no additional cost and gives the parties the opportunity to avoid further time and expense if unnecessary in light of investigation to date.

The other optional step is an **expedited appeal** of the final decision. To invoke this, a party promptly notifies the administering service or Neutrals of the intent to appeal after receiving the final decision. The appeal is conducted according to a provision in the agreed rules covering appeal costs, timeliness, and selection of at least two additional **Reviewing Neutrals** to reexamine the investigation and conclusions of the original Neutrals. If necessary, the reviewing neutrals can supplement any earlier-requested-but-refused investigation which they believe is warranted. Finally, *all* Neutrals vote whether and how to change the final decision. This enables a rapid review and an effective layer of security against the risk of serious error in the original final decision due to undisclosed or unrecognized bias or other apparent shortcoming on the part of the original Neutrals.

In my preferred version of the appeal step, the cost is borne entirely by the appealing party—regardless of outcome—as it otherwise unduly penalizes the original prevailing party. Appeal, therefore, would and should be undertaken only if the appealing party strongly believes that the error is so clearly egregious, and the outcome so important, that it is worth the added cost and time to believe that two additional reasonable, unbiased reviewers will agree and correct the decision if given the opportunity. By forcing a dissatisfied party to "put their money where their mouth is," frivolous or tactical appeals are discouraged, while gross injustices may be prevented.

Figure 7 illustrates the three basic and two optional steps in the NDR process.

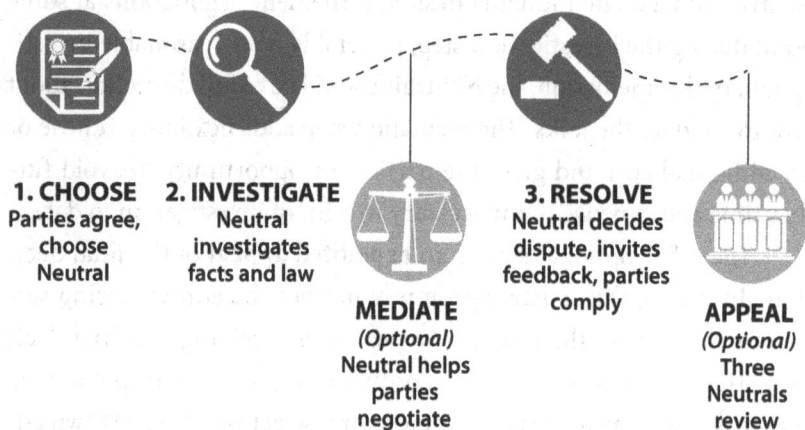

FIGURE 7 Neutral-Driven Resolution (NDR) 3 Basic and 2 Optional Steps.

1. CHOOSE
Parties agree, choose Neutral

2. INVESTIGATE
Neutral investigates facts and law

MEDIATE
(Optional)
Neutral helps parties negotiate

3. RESOLVE
Neutral decides dispute, invites feedback, parties comply

APPEAL
(Optional)
Three Neutrals review

HOW MUCH CAN BE SAVED?

Projecting and measuring the savings from using NDR are not difficult. *Legal costs* alone should fall between three (3) to six (6) *times* lower, *per party*—in other words, between 1/6 and 1/3 of what they would be in lawyer-driven process. Yes, that's correct. It's *that much less, every time.* This is based on simple logic, experience to date, analyses of attorney litigation bills, litigation cost rules of thumb, and anecdotal evidence—all without known dispute.

BRIEF

One might think that the known very low costs of small claims court would make it easy to measure savings from using NDR, but the role and rules governing small claims judges do not encompass those of a true proactive investigator, nor is there reported data on the time spent by those judges and their staffs on such cases.

The easiest way to see and understand this in a measurable way is to analyze litigation legal bills. These bills routinely disclose that *at most* one of *every* three billed hours (and dollars) are focused on truth-seeking activity, while *at least* two of every three hours (and dollars) are focused on procedural compliance, coordination, maneuver, or formal advocacy. That's arguably fine when the stakes are high enough to justify it, but not when all those additional hours are billed in a case worth less than each party's legal costs. Moreover, because opposing legal teams in any dispute essentially must *duplicate* and counter each other's efforts, their separate efforts at truth-seeking are largely redundant despite their opposing perspectives.

BRIEF

Some will argue that separate, opposing efforts are *not* redundant, *because* of the parties' differences in perspectives, which lead to additional truthful revelations and/or competing versions of what is true, but the model here already fully accounts for this. It builds in the additional time spent by each side in factual and legal investigation of the *opposing side's version* of what is true.

SIDEBAR

In my early investigation of the limited stakes challenge, I examined numerous legal bills with itemized task and time entries provided by different lawyers and their clients to determine how much time was devoted to truth-seeking vs. other necessary tasks in litigation.

If an entry focused on factual or substantive legal investigation and analysis, I classified it as truth-seeking. Entries not so focused—for example, those dealing with scheduling, coordination, maneuver, procedural research, formal advocacy, and the like—were not put in this category. Many entries, of course, were hybrids, requiring subjective judgment and allocation. I was looking for answers, not vindication of a hypothesis, so I took care to credit at least portions of most entries involving formal discovery and brief-writing as having a truth-seeking aspect, even if it was apparent that much of the time was spent on objections or procedural arguments.

The findings were extraordinarily consistent—regardless of lawyer, type of case, etc. I welcome (and hope to assist) a future study by a reputable organization following a more scientifically disciplined approach using larger samples. However, the findings were so clear, and so readily corroborated by anecdotal accounts from attorneys, personal experience, and the conceptual thinking around the subject, that I'm confident any objective study will bear out the essential allocations in the text.

Consequently, an NDR process that focuses almost all time on truth-seeking stands to save at least 2/3 of total effort (i.e., the non-truth-seeking part) spent in litigation and its equivalents. If the work that remains to be done (the truth-seeking part) is consolidated into one neutral person or team (instead of two opposing teams), that 1/3 may be roughly cut in half. This reduces the total time and effort need-ed for a neutral-driven resolution of comparable investigative and analytical quality to about 1/6 of its lawyer-driven alternative. **Figure 8** illustrates this equation using the *Why Litigation Costs So Much* pie chart from Chapter 2. Further, if neutral-driven process preempts even one party or lawyer from additional wasteful, ill-advised, or abusive behavior, the savings increase even more.

FIGURE 8 Comparison: Why Litigation Costs so Much vs. NDR's Potential for Savings.

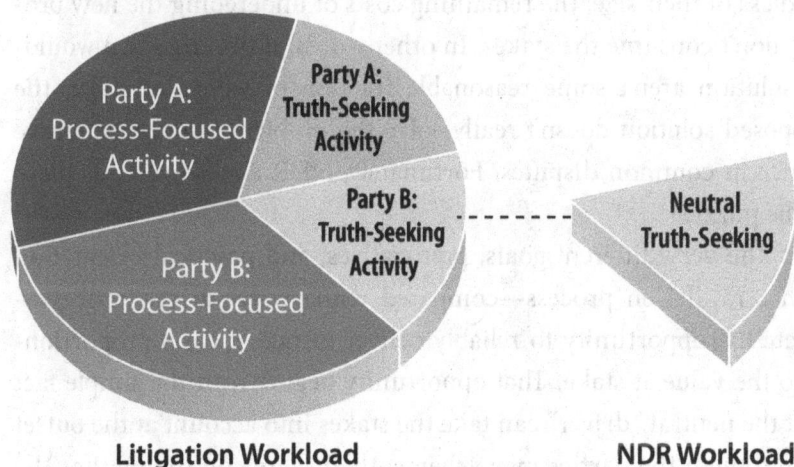

Litigation Workload   NDR Workload

Conversely, any unaccounted-for factor or reality that adds to the expense of NDR reduces the savings. One example of such additional expense would be legal fees paid by one side for their attorney's advice during the process. This expense, however valuable, typically makes up only a tiny fraction of legal fees billed in litigation, and should be reduced even more in the context of a neutral-driven process. Moreover, when the potential for savings is as large as described, there's room to accommodate such additional expense and any other extenuating circumstances—real or imagined—and still make the case for using this approach from the perspectives of legal costs savings, economic rationality, and reliable quality of outcome.

Finally, we shouldn't forget that the above construct accounts *only* for savings in legal fees and costs, and not the additional and similarly substantial savings in the very real and substantial *hidden* costs that also accompany adversarial process.

BUT COULD IT STILL COST TOO MUCH?

The costs savings of any solution also need to be enough so that, regardless of their size, the remaining costs of undergoing the new process don't consume the stakes. In other words, if the costs of a would-be solution aren't some reasonable fraction of what's at stake, the proposed solution doesn't really solve the problem of over-expensive justice in common disputes. Fortunately, NDR also solves this piece of the puzzle.

The very different goals, prerogatives, and practical orientation of neutral-driven process—compared with lawyer-driven process—create the opportunity to reliably deliver justice at costs proportional to the value at stake. That opportunity begins with the simple fact that the neutral "driver" can take the stakes into account at the outset even though the parties may vehemently disagree on the merits. The Neutral is free to adjust the tasks and fairly distribute the workload so that they make economic sense, i.e., their cost is a reasonable fraction of those stakes. For example, reasonable people can presumably agree that a $10,000 dispute doesn't warrant $20,000 in costly effort when an effort costing only $3,000 or $4,000 is highly likely to reach roughly the same result.

Neutrals who are *proactive* investigators/decision-makers also can learn quickly and reliably at the outset what kinds and sources of information are needed and available to justly resolve the dispute. They can then estimate with relatively high confidence the effort to be undertaken and what they will need to charge the parties to complete the task—*unlike a traditional judge limited to reacting to opposing attorney moves and countermoves.*

Provided the investigating Neutrals are experienced and skilled, they generally shouldn't have to worry about unforeseen initiatives by attorneys or parties that may dramatically lengthen or disrupt the time and path to resolution, though they should have flexibility to address any important unforeseen circumstance. Indeed, if a responsible administrative provider of the NDR process explicitly directs all Neutral candidates to engage in the exercise described in this paragraph and then commit to a fixed or not-to-exceed fee based on this process, then proportionality is assured and the legitimate and overall best interests of all participants in efficiency will be fully aligned. This is a far cry from what our current system delivers.

LET'S ALSO LOSE THE HIDDEN COSTS

Big savings in legal fees and other direct out-of-pocket costs are absolutely necessary, but they are not the only costs that a true solution must address. I've already alluded to the "hidden costs" of litigation—very real costs that are usually ignored and seldom accounted for by lawyers and their clients in litigation decision-making. These are difficult and often uncomfortable for the players to identify and measure. Such ambiguities, however, don't make these substantial costs go away; rather, a bright light needs to be cast on them.

Every hour spent by an individual party, CEO, manager, in-house counsel, supervisor, accounting clerk, line worker, etc. on litigation is money, time, energy, focus, and opportunity diverted from productivity—regardless of outcome. A nominal portion of that spend may be potentially returned through valuable lessons or some other gain, but the rest is truly lost productivity for each person affected. The best approximation of this productivity cost is probably the compensation rate paid each of those individuals when working, multiplied by the number of hours they are forced to divert to the lawsuit. That's simply $X/hour x Y hours of distraction. Just as these hours are considered and estimated to determine projected profitability at the beginning of a business relationship or contract, they deserve to be separately accounted for and estimated as likely cost items (whether incremental or as overhead) and added to any projected legal fees and other costs at the beginning of every legal dispute.

FIGURE 9 Hidden Costs of Litigation Add Up.

DESCRIPTION	CALCULATION	VALUE/ COST ($)
Lost Productivity		
Senior Officer/GM	50 hours x $200/hour	10,000
Asst. Dept. Manager	80 hours x $75/hour	6,000
Line Employee Witness	25 hours x $20/hour	500
	SUBTOTAL	$16,500
Risk to Valued Relationship or Reputation	10% risk of loss x $50,000 value of future net profits	5,000
Stress and Anxiety	What would pay to avoid	1,000
	TOTAL	$22,500

Figure 9 illustrates a hypothetical calculation of a lawsuit's hidden costs. Lost productivity alone adds up to $16,500, *win or lose*, for an organization likely to incur the following:

- A minimal 50 hours of lost productivity at $200 per hour for a Senior Officer or Manager strategizing with lawyers, monitoring case progress, leading negotiations, and testifying,

- *Plus* 80 hours at $75 per hour by an Assistant Department Manager reviewing multiple sets of records requests and coordinating collection and responses with an attorney,

- *Plus* 25 hours at $20 per hour by a line employee who, as a key witness, will undergo witness interviews, deposition preparation, deposition testimony, and transcript review and correction.

Conceptually, the estimate should be increased further by a probability factor for likely underestimating such distractions, based on the same reasoning discussed in Chapter 4 when projecting future legal fees in a dispute.

Similarly, as **Figure 9** indicates, some accounting, however rough, can be made of the value of the additional risk of losing a relationship or suffering some loss of reputation because emotions may escalate or perspectives diverge further *during* the dispute process. One simple, but meaningful way of doing that is to multiply a rough estimate of the net value to the estimator of the relationship, reputation, or other "asset" at risk by a fraction equal to the likelihood of losing that value due to the litigation. For example, using such probability analysis, the hidden cost of a 10% risk of losing a business relationship valued at $50,000 in net profit could be estimated at $5,000.

A third real and roughly measurable hidden cost is the additional harmful stress and anxiety that involved individuals will suffer while the dispute is pending.[1] To estimate this, consider what one would be willing to pay simply to avoid it. Although this is a purely subjective measure and there's some risk that it could overlap other hidden costs, just contemplating and assigning value is enlightening and sobering.

Fortunately, there's a silver lining to the cloud of hidden costs: While the nature of these costs makes them *unavoidable* in *adversarial* process, they are largely *mitigated in a neutral-driven* process. Productivity losses are slashed when the method of investigation and resolution makes efficient use of people's time and doesn't indulge in formal and competitive opportunities to impose burdens, assert rights, and retaliate for perceived offense. Similarly, the risks of exacerbating already strained relationships and triggering costly ego-and-emotion-driven behaviors are marginalized in a cooperative process run by an investigating Neutral decision-maker who serves as buffer for, and cooler-headed interpreter of, the words and actions of parties or their attorneys. Finally, these differences can deliver relative dignity and peace of mind about, and acceptance of, both the process and its outcome—whatever that outcome may be.

So, does NDR really work like it should? Where does and doesn't it fit? And how do we get it? The next chapters answer these questions.

CHAPTER SUMMARY

- NDR consists of three simple, basic steps.

- First, the parties *choose and agree*, in writing, to use NDR. Parties with an existing business or other relationship may agree to do so before any dispute arises, as is often done via contract clauses to arbitrate or mediate future disputes. This agreement is naturally much more difficult to reach in disputes that arise between strangers and/or after a dispute arises. Any agreement to use NDR should at least specify whether the outcome will be binding (strongly preferred) and identify a neutral service provider and/or a set of fair process rules and principles.

- Ideally, the service provider vets candidate Neutrals for the parties and commits to a total fixed fee that is proportional to the financial stakes.

- Second, the agreed Neutrals *proactively investigate* the pertinent facts and law in order to find the truth and decide the dispute accordingly. If a party lies or fails to cooperate fully and promptly, the Neutrals may hold this against the offender.

- Third, the Neutrals decide the dispute in writing. If a party fails to comply with a binding decision, it should be enforceable in court with that party obligated to pay all fees and costs of both the NDR process and enforcement.

- Ideally, the Neutrals first issue a preliminary or tentative decision and invite the parties to react and comment. This may reveal mistakes that persuade the Neutrals to reopen the investigation or change the decision.

- Two optional steps can be added if desired. One is mediation, where the Neutrals help the parties try to negotiate a settlement before making a decision. The other is an expedited appeal to additional Neutrals, with the appealing party paying the costs.

- The basic NDR process delivers huge out-of-pocket savings to both sides, reducing legal fees and related costs *between three and six times* compared with litigation and assuring that total costs are a reasonable fraction of what is at stake.

- Unlike litigation, NDR also has very low *hidden* costs. These real and measurable costs include the value of each side's distracted time for testifying, finding and reviewing records, consulting with attorneys, etc. They also include the risks of losing a relationship, suffering loss of reputation, and experiencing unhealthy stress and anxiety.

"I see. And precisely what methods did you use to determine that my client was a 'bad boy'?"

CHAPTER 7

DOES THE GLOVE FIT?

"If the glove doesn't fit, you must acquit." These famous words by trial attorney Johnnie Cochran in the infamous OJ Simpson trial also have fair application here: This book indicts attorney-driven adversarial process—*and NOT attorneys in general*—as the main cause of a huge and growing civil justice gap in common disputes, and proposes NDR as a real answer to the problem. If, however, NDR doesn't really *fit* our criteria for better, more rational justice in limited stakes disputes, then let's not convict the accused nor waste our time with a false solution. Even if NDR *does meet* our criteria, it will not be a good fit in every situation. So, before we get too excited, let's compare how NDR impacts the key criteria and assess where it does and doesn't fit.

For brevity and convenience, let's consolidate our solution criteria and NDR's impact into four critical elements:

Quality Control—Our courts are imperfect, but the weight of evidence suggests that they decide civil cases correctly and fairly on the merits—in other words, they "get it right"—about 90% of the time, even without accounting for reversals through appeals.[1] So, any solution to the justice gap problem must assure reasonably comparable quality. While NDR is too new to offer statistical comparison, there is every reason to believe that it does achieve this level of quality control. First off, it retains critical elements of judicial process that assure robust truth-seeking, fairness, and reliability. Like our court system, NDR:

- Enables thorough investigation of the facts and law

- Enables review loops that can fix mistakes and bias

- Gives parties a say in who will control, investigate, and decide their disagreement

- Assures all parties a full opportunity to be heard

- Can incorporate mediation and other situational flexibility

- Gives neutral(s) authority to compel cooperation and make findings binding

- Accommodates lawyer advice and involvement (though limited)

Then NDR discards only noncritical elements and influences, which on balance tend not to make enough difference in truth-seeking to justify their high costs, susceptibility to abuse, and process proliferation.

SIDEBAR

What About Juries and Cross-Examination?

NDR neither assures opportunity for formal advocacy such as sworn cross-examination of a lying or biased witness by opposing counsel, nor preserves a right to jury trial. Many fine trial attorneys and other students of our judicial system may be quick to disagree with my suggestion that these hallowed tools are "noncritical" in limited stakes disputes.

To be sure, effective cross-examination and jury trial can sometimes make big differences in outcome, and we attorneys revel in, long remember, and love to tell our war stories about those occasions. The problem is that these tools are extraordinarily expensive and time-consuming in preparation and execution, so they are hard-pressed when stakes are modest to make a cost-justified difference in the search for truth—especially when a skilled, intelligent decision-maker already is empowered to find that truth. Moreover, these tools also are prone to their own risks of bias and clever abuse.

Meanwhile, NDR offers certain advantages in quality control—improvements even—over the judicial system. These include:

- The ability of the parties to mutually select investigating Neutrals who also are subject matter experts

- A more level playing field where uneven wealth, resources, and sympathy offer little, if any, advantage

- Delivery of a fair process and principled resolution in a much shorter time

Costs/Savings—Replacing the formal tools, procedures, duplication of effort, and competitiveness of opposing teams with a practical, neutral-controlled investigation enables tremendous efficiency gains and makes the size and likely duration of the Neutral's workload predictable. This hugely reduces both out-of-pocket and hidden costs to a proportional, affordable, cooperative, speedy, and truth-focused exercise. In addition, asking Neutral candidates who know the stakes and have expertise in the subject to quote and compete for NDR assignments on a fixed-or-capped-fee basis assures that these efficiency gains are passed on to the parties.

> *When attorneys know they won't be actively driving the prosecution or defense of a claim beyond initial consultation, negotiation, or ongoing strategic advice, this substantially realigns their best interests with—and no longer against—those of their clients in terms of speed and efficiency of resolution, and value for service.*

Alignment—Relegating attorneys to advisor-only roles greatly limits the need, opportunity, and incentives for fee-generating activity. Moreover, when attorneys know they won't be actively driving the prosecution or defense of a claim beyond initial consultation, negotiation, or ongoing strategic advice, this substantially *realigns* their best interests *with*—and no longer *against*—those of their clients in terms of speed and efficiency of resolution, and value for service. Similarly, consolidating dispute investigation, facilitation, and decision in one Neutral person or team working on a fixed-fee or capped-fee basis aligns the interests of these service providers with all parties in a speedy, efficient, and value-based process. Finally, in those situations where one party's skills in storytelling or gamesmanship are superior, or where one party relies on an attorney as spokesperson/liaison, the NDR Neutral's inherent responsibility to recognize this and not allow one side to take unfair advantage is the same as that of a courtroom judge. However, the NDR Neutral has the distinct advantage of not having to suffer attorney "demands" for records, depositions, motions, briefs of issues, and other "rights" inherent in adversarial process.

Psychological Needs—By keeping critical features of our judicial system, NDR satisfies our deep psychological and cultural drives for a process and outcome that both sides can accept. Meanwhile, disallowing expensive, noncritical features enables the efficiency gains that parties need in order to get real justice. Other psychological benefits of NDR include reduced rage and other emotional triggering, lower stress, less distraction, greater dignity, greater opportunity to salvage valuable relationships or even enhance reputations, and a potentially more satisfying sense of direct involvement and transparency.

In sum, NDR compares favorably with other paths to resolution across many decision factors, as revealed in **Figure 10**, which adds a new column to the Comparison Table first introduced in Chapter 3.

FIGURE 10 Comparison of Leading Dispute Resolution Methods and NDR.

Deciding Factors	Dispute Resolution Methods				
	Litigation	Arbitration	Mediation	Negotiation	**NDR**
1. Do costs make sense?	−	−	?	+	+
2. Are costs fixed or open/ variable?	−	−	−	−	+
3. Reasonably fast process?	−	−	?	+	+

Deciding Factors	Dispute Resolution Methods				
	Litigation	Arbitration	Mediation	Negotiation	NDR
4. Does not require parties to agree?	+	−	−	−	−
5. Can a disappointed party appeal?	+	−	NA	NA	+
6. Is discovery robust *and* efficient?	−	−	?	−	+
7. Potential to save a relationship?	−	−	+	+	+
8. Sets precedent for any later disputes?	+	+	?	?	?
9. Stays private?	−	+	+	+	+
10. Is it fair?	+	+	+	?	+

Legend: " + " good, " − " bad, " ? " depends on situation, " NA " not applicable

PERFECT FITS

In fact, NDR is a particularly perfect fit for a wide range of limited stakes disputes.

Common commercial disputes are a natural fit—whether or not someone made an honest mistake (such as a warehouse worker miscounting the number of boxes on a truck) or is trying to take unfair advantage (when a repair person exaggerates the number of hours to charge). These can be important disputes that make the difference between profit or loss—failure or success—so they may demand real justice, but the stakes usually are not high enough to warrant the time, costs, and collateral damage of the legal equivalent of war. Meanwhile, once identified, the legal and factual issues of common commercial disputes tend to lend themselves to straightforward investigation and analysis. All these considerations together make these disputes natural candidates for NDR.

Business partner, start-up investment, and real estate transaction disputes measured in five- to low six-figure stakes would gain from a fair and reliable process that respects and preserves precious capital and may prevent further damage to important relationships. One subset of these that immediately comes to mind for residential realtors is the common post-sale claim of failure to disclose material facts about the property to the buyer. These claims, whether valid or not, routinely vex brokers, sellers, and buyers alike because it only takes one irrational (or conniving) actor to quickly force all parties into a no-win scenario that unfairly robs the innocent of valuable time and money. These disputes are so common and wasteful that many states mandate or encourage special dispute resolution processes for them, few of which approach the fairness and efficiency of NDR.

The prospect of real and economic justice finds equal attraction in **everyday noncommercial disputes** as well, for example, between neighbors over things like fences and boundaries, or family members settling an estate or probate issue that is emotionally charged or otherwise threatens to consume much of the estate's value. Similarly, just as collaborative lawyers have made considerable inroads in amicably settling divorces, so, too, can NDR prove of great value in that context, although emotions run so high and perceptions of fairness vary so deeply here that greed and impulses to punish or "get even" are often difficult to overcome irrespective of the forum.

Construction and other time-sensitive disputes should benefit greatly from the potential lightning speed and reliability of NDR, since domino delays can turn small disputes into large consequences that destroy already-thin margins. Moreover, if the economically more powerful party in construction contracts can accept that surrendering some of its inherent strong-arm leverage is likely to be offset by faster vindications and gains in reputation as a quality business partner, then use of the method should boom in construction.

Insureds and insurers both stand to benefit from using NDR, but for different reasons. Insureds legitimately want to know they are receiving fair claims treatment, prompt resolution, and full value for their paid premiums—all of which NDR can help deliver. Meanwhile, today's best insurers want to minimize aggregate, company-wide costs and payouts of claims while building the best possible brands for quality of service and value. An innovation that dramatically slashes outside legal fee budgets (and probably enhances in-house claims handling efficiency) for comparable or smaller total payouts, *and* improves customer service satisfaction, stands to serve insurers' bottom lines *and* their reputations. NDR can be either mandatory or optional in insurance contracts or an available solution for claims adjusters to offer insureds and third-party claimants.

BRIEF

This begs the question, **"What about insurers whose claims adjustment policies are unenlightened and reflect old-school resistance?"** The answer is that the speed and prevalence of product and service reviews in the 21st century doom these dinosaurs, whose extinction will accelerate if they fail to adapt and promote customer-centric practices like NDR.

In sum, NDR can be a sorely needed win-win for reason and honesty in insurance claims practice—equally protecting insureds (from delays, hard-ball negotiating, and other unfair insurer practices) *and* insurers (from bloated, outrageous, and fraudulent claims). Experimental programs would quickly reveal the extent of such net gains to both sides as claimants and insureds forego legal threats and litigation in favor of truly independent, fair, and fast investigations and decisions when standard claims adjustment efforts prove inadequate.

Even **employment disputes**—that bastion of emotionally triggered overreaction by employees and employers alike—would see far more real justice. Aggrieved employees have the right to fair treatment and resolution without delay or undue cost, and this is what most of them really want. However, they naturally don't trust their employers' objectivity to deliver it. Similarly, the vast majority of employers actually want, and are entitled to, the same thing, not necessarily because it's right—though that's reason enough for many—but because it's less costly than resisting, denying, and ultimately paying for good claims. That's true both in terms of out-of-pocket dollars paid for injury, legal fees, regulatory penalties, etc., and hidden costs due to lost productivity and work culture fallout. The biggest challenges for employers dealing with employee disputes are:

- Sorting out fact from fiction (especially where investigation usually involves, and the outcome may affect, other employees)

- Properly implementing and documenting investigations, interim conditions, and final resolutions

- Not paying false claims or overpaying weak claims, where doing so sets a precedent that invites even more such claims in the future

Because it's fast, inexpensive, and driven by an outside and independent Neutral, NDR readily meets the above-described legitimate needs of both employees and employers in most limited stakes disputes. At present, because of unsettled and politically charged rules and debates in many states over how to assure adequate protection of employees' rights, probably the best ways to introduce NDR into employment relationships are for employers to offer it in employee handbooks and employment contracts as an "optional" or "voluntary" method (probably employer-paid) for resolving appropriate disputes that may arise in the employment relationship, and for counsel on both sides in disputes simply to "take the high road" and suggest it.

International disputes should welcome NDR with open arms. Foreign businesses absolutely despise what they perceive to be the costly arrogance of the American judicial system. Other cultures often are more economically pragmatic in their handling of legal disputes—either explicitly or implicitly acting to assure that costs bear a rational relationship to stakes. Some of these cultures, like China, so extol harmonious business relations and renounce adversarial confrontation as loutish behavior that their laws and governments will not enforce American judgments against their citizens and their business corporations (who are also loathe to settle disputes based on Western-style exaggerated demands and threats). NDR's non-adversarial, principled, inexpensive, and dignified process should have cross-border appeal as it aligns the interests of all despite their different cultural perspectives.

> *International disputes should welcome NDR with open arms. Foreign businesses absolutely despise what they perceive to be the costly arrogance of the American judicial system.*

NDR also should have a role—perhaps a very large one— in shrinking the **"access to justice" gap faced by the poor**. A June 2017 report from the Legal Services Corporation asserts that while 71% of low-income American households experienced at least one civil legal problem in the year prior, an appalling 86% of the problems reported received inadequate or no legal help.[2] Making matters worse, these are not primarily business problems, but more typically fundamental well-being and quality of life issues over health care, housing conditions, disability access, veterans' benefits, and domestic violence.[3] Many of these situations absolutely require pro bono (free for those who qualify) or very low-cost legal advice and, sometimes, adversarial representation. To the extent the situations fall into any of the categories and rationales of perfect fits for NDR described above, the low cost, efficiency, speed, level playing field, and reliability of NDR can make a major difference for good in this grossly underserved and compelling segment of the civil justice gap.

Eventually, even non-catastrophic **professional malpractice claims**—medical, legal, and other—could be resolved in a fraction of the time and cost in a simple, private, and principled neutral-driven process of truth-seeking. NDR naturally lends itself to opportunities for creative reconciliation, including a confidential environment where an important *mea culpa* or apology, when appropriate, could be delivered without reputation-damaging consequences or expanded liability risk.

Finally, NDR can effectively serve the cause of just resolution even in **very large disputes**. Here, adversarial legal teams (and even individual parties) can choose it as a form of **proactive early neutral evaluation (ENE)** that may lead to settlement or, at a minimum, may better inform future strategy and action. NDR can even incorporate an efficient and inexpensive mock jury or focus group exercise in disputes that ultimately may turn on a jury's verdict. At least one company, Yurjury (www.yurjury.com), already offers this very tool for use in NDR processes.

The list above is illustrative, not exhaustive. Client-centric lawyers and enlightened businesses and individuals in virtually any endeavor will come to find NDR a valuable tool in the disputes in which it makes economic sense for all concerned.

SOMETIMES THE SOLUTION IS NOT NDR

While NDR is an important solution to the limited stakes justice gap, I recognize that it is not right for *all* situations. Having flexibility in our spectrum of legal solutions is mission critical. Here are examples of when NDR *does not* fit:

- **When the parties, *before* starting down the lawsuit path, can voluntarily share enough information and open-mindedness to settle on some principled and mutually dignified basis—** whether with or without the help of lawyers.

- **When perceived stakes are so high that adversarial process is worth its many costs.** Without limiting the possibilities, this category probably includes disputes over high dollar values, critical intellectual property rights, "bet-the-company" existential disputes, threatened loss of professional licensing necessary to pursue a livelihood, as well as child custody, domestic violence, and comparable family law disputes.

- **When a crime is charged.** Our criminal law courts have the potential to impose punishments ranging from fines to incarceration—and even death in some jurisdictions. Upholding an accused's rights to a fair trial, a jury of one's peers, proof beyond a reasonable doubt, and a vigorous defense are fundamental constitutional rights in this context. While NDR can deliver a fair, unbiased, and equitable forum in civil disputes over money-measurable value, criminal cases are by their nature almost always high stakes matters involving life or liberty, so the appropriate venue must usually be the court system.

- **When an indispensable third party or nonparty witness will not cooperate.** Only courtroom judges and other statutorily authorized officers like arbitrators can issue subpoenas to compel uncooperative nonparties to testify or produce records in a legal dispute. NDR, which is legally only a form of settlement between parties who agree to use the process, does not *at this time* have such authority. If critical evidence is unavailable from third parties, NDR may not be a good solution.

- **When a party needs *immediate* equitable (non-money) relief that has the force of law**—such as a temporary restraining order or preliminary injunction. Only a court can issue such an order.

- **When considerations of public policy prevent otherwise willing parties from effectively agreeing to NDR.** For example, legislators tend to be so solicitous of the rights of those perceived as disadvantaged in American society that consumer, employment, and other laws often discourage or prevent such persons from availing themselves of fair, efficient, and practical process *outside* the adversarial system.

- **When one side simply won't agree to NDR for whatever reasons**—whether from baser motives like greed, vengeance, advantage, or power, or relatively innocent causes, such as unfamiliarity, mistrust, or mistaken judgment. This is especially likely in tort (e.g., injury) claims and other disputes between or among strangers, or in marital and family law disputes (because of high emotional or financial stakes). Finally, NDR will not work in any relationship where one side is inherently suspicious (or *counseled* to be suspicious) of *anything* the other side might suggest.

As the above bullet list suggests, enough legal disputes still require traditional lawyer-driven process that NDR, even with all its advantages, will remove only a modest percentage of the total number of cases from the courts. On the other hand, this book shows that most civil (i.e., noncriminal) legal actions in the United States are fought over limited money stakes and end up consuming most or all of those stakes in excessive legal fees, related expenses, and hidden costs. Consequently, whenever parties and their counsel in limited money stakes situations can agree at the outset of a relationship or dispute to try NDR on for size, there is every reason to believe that the fit will be good—delivering more real justice and satisfaction to the parties, *and* to their client-centric counsel.

CHAPTER SUMMARY

- NDR fits the criteria for better, more rational justice in limited stakes disputes, with quality comparable to going to court. It saves the parties time, money, and stress, while aligning the best interests of attorneys, clients, and Neutrals alike. It also satisfies the parties' deep psychological and cultural drives for an acceptable process and outcome.

- NDR is a perfect fit for a wide range of common monetary disputes. Examples include commercial contracts, business partnerships, start-up investments, common real estate transactions, will probates, neighbor conflicts, divorce asset settlements, time-sensitive claims (like construction contractor-subcontractor), insurance claims, employer-employee, international, access to justice for the poor, professional malpractice, and even early neutral evaluation of larger disputes.

- NDR admittedly is *not* a good fit in all situations. These include high stakes disputes, such as intellectual property rights, "bet-the-company" existential disputes, child custody, threats to livelihood like loss of professional licensing, domestic violence, and criminal charges. NDR is also unlikely to make sense in situations where a key third party will not cooperate, a judicial restraining order or injunction is needed, or honest parties are able to negotiate an early, amicable, and principled settlement rather than submit to *any* formal process. Finally, NDR isn't viable where one side simply won't agree to it, and where victim protection laws may prohibit it.

CHAPTER 8

BUT DOES NDR REALLY WORK?

The last three chapters introduced NDR and made the case that this is a real solution to the civil justice gap. But does NDR *really* work?

World history is chock-full of wonderful sounding inventions and innovations that in fact simply haven't delivered. From Clark Stanley's original Snake Oil Liniment (1880s) to daylight-watchable motion pictures (circa 1910), from hand-dipped electrified water for curing headaches (about 1920) to RJ Reynolds' smokeless cigarettes (1980s), and from New Coke (1985) to Theranos' recent infamous blood-testing technology (2015)—many highly touted problem-solvers either have failed spectacularly or turned out to be complete frauds. It's often only when we apply promising innovations in practice to real people in real situations that we find out whether they meet their promise or have overlooked some critical fact.

Fortunately, the simple model for NDR described in this book and the claim of its extraordinary effectiveness are neither merely conceptual nor fictional. NDR works—exactly as advertised, and in multiple contexts. It's here, now, and available for most limited stakes disputes in which the parties understand that they otherwise will grossly overpay in every way for "justice" delivered through litigation and its most popular "ADR" substitutes.

Following are true, real-world stories illustrating exactly how disagreeing parties have used NDR in each of five different common situations to win real justice.

BRIEF

As use of the method grows and evolves, it's my hope that readers who have had, or come to have, experience with NDR will share their stories with me and perhaps even allow me to share them publicly. To that end, my personal email address for this purpose is rob.christopher@justresolve.com, or contact@justresolve.com.

THE CASE OF THE CONTRACTOR WHO JUMPED THE GUN

The testing laboratory introduced in this book's first chapter was an early adopter of NDR, largely because of the frustrating experience described there.

The year was 2013. Despite performing hundreds of contracts annually without issue, the lab again faced a customer dispute. The California-based lab and its Massachusetts customer hotly disputed the lab's reimbursement claim for expenses and contractually specified **liquidated damages** for time-sensitive costs that had to be incurred a second time by the laboratory because the customer delayed the start of a scheduled project. Fortunately for both sides, the parties' contractual dispute resolution clause specified binding NDR (instead of court or arbitration) for any dispute arising out of the contract, because the contract was only for $100,000 of services. At stake was about $28,000, but it was an important sum in terms of profitability to the laboratory and capital budget to the study-sponsoring customer.

The lab informed the customer and the NDR neutral service provider (administrator) of the claim.[1] The NDR provider interviewed both parties about what had happened, what facts and information they believed were important, and each party's concerns and wants. The provider then found and vetted a mutually acceptable Neutral—a senior law professor from a reputable midwestern university with industry subject matter experience. The Neutral quoted a *fixed* dollar amount below $1,500 per party to receive and review the records, personally interview the witnesses, research applicable legal principles, mediate the dispute if possible, and decide it if necessary in a written judgment with explanation, all according to the administering service provider's NDR rules.

The complete investigation and mediation effort took only three weeks. When mediation failed, within days the Neutral issued his tentative decision and analysis for comment, and then issued an identical Final Decision, which neither party challenged. The laboratory lost on the merits—the Neutral's detailed review and analysis revealed that the lab had jumped the gun on making time-sensitive expenditures and failed to comply with its own express contractual pre-conditions to recovering damages for a sponsor's delayed start to the study.

The laboratory was naturally disappointed in the outcome, but was grateful for the fair process and low cost to learn its mistake—lower than what it would have paid to have legal counsel fully explore and assess its claim, and several times lower than it would have cost to mediate, arbitrate, or litigate the claim. The customer/study sponsor was delighted with its vindication and the modest costs in money and distracted time to get there—costs much lower and a net outcome much better and faster compared to retaining and consulting legal counsel to defend the claim. Meanwhile, the parties were able to proceed with the planned study on a later timetable and thereby preserve both their relationship and most of the benefits of their bargain. The NDR service provider later conducted a quality control legal audit of the Neutral's process, evidence, analysis, and decision, finding that the Neutral's work was appropriate and correct.

There's a telling sequel to this story as well. About a year later, there was a subsequent breach of contract dispute of similar size—about $27,000—involving the same testing lab and a different customer. The customer, however—through its outside litigation counsel—refused to proceed with NDR despite the contract's mandate. Due to cost considerations, the lab chose not to try to enforce the clause in court, except to assert an additional claim for the lost benefit of the bargain to use NDR. In other words, the laboratory asked for separate breach of contract damages in the amount of *all the additional costs* it would incur to resolve the underlying dispute in court. The parties then spent a year in litigation, spent more than $30,000 *each* in legal fees, and finally reached a compromise settlement before trial. The laboratory's attorney adroitly used the NDR breach claim to negotiate a better compromise, but since the case never went to court, the only real winners were the lawyers.

TAKEAWAY: THEY WHO ANTICIPATE, WIN

As the above case study suggests, whenever possible, the ideal time for people or entities to agree to use NDR is at the outset of their relationship, before any dispute has arisen. At that time, optimism and mutual trust are highest, and no one of good faith expects troublesome future disputes. Nevertheless, most people know that, even with the best of intentions, misunderstandings that defy quick and fair resolution can visit anyone. Consequently, most written contracts today—and many related writings containing relational terms and conditions like purchase orders, confirmations, invoices, employee handbooks, etc.—include dispute resolution clauses that contemplate this possibility and lay out how the parties wish to manage their relationship in the unlikely event that a dispute does arise. Otherwise, their default remedy is to go to court. Fortunately, with few exceptions, parties in a business or other relationship have the right and freedom to knowingly agree *in writing and in advance* to any reasonable alternative dispute resolution process. The complete range of alternatives and particulars for these contract clauses are beyond the scope of this book, other than to mention that, at least in the United States, the two most commonly specified ADR methods are arbitration and mediation.

A clause designating NDR is very similar. Like a clause designating arbitration or mediation, it specifies a fair and reasonable out-of-court settlement method, and such alternative methods and settlements are generally both favored and enforced by our courts.[2] Moreover, NDR may also qualify for ready enforcement as a form of arbitration where it meets statutory criteria.

In common contracts where the parties recognize that *any* conceivable dispute would involve only limited stakes, a short-form NDR dispute resolution clause could read simply as follows:

> **DISPUTE RESOLUTION**. The parties agree to submit any dispute arising out of or relating to this Agreement to independent neutral service _____[e.g., "Just Resolve LLC (www.justresolve.com)"] for *binding* neutral-driven, non-adversarial resolution ("NDR") according to its then-current rules.

Many contracts, however, may require or justify longer, more detailed provisions in order to comply with local or governing law, add additional terms, or simply clarify the parties' intentions. For example, in some contracts the parties may wish to specify NDR for limited stakes disputes while reserving traditional methods for high stakes or complex disputes. In this two-tiered situation, the parties usually need only agree on the dollar amount that will be the dividing line between *limited* and *high* stakes disputes. Such a clause might read as follows:

> **DISPUTE RESOLUTION**. The parties agree to submit any dispute arising out of or relating to this Agreement to independent neutral service _____ [e.g., "Just Resolve LLC (www.justresolve.com)"] for *binding* neutral-driven, non-adversarial resolution ("NDR") according to its then-current rules, *if* the amount in controversy, as believed by the parties or the NDR service, is less than or equal to _____ [e.g., "$250,000"]. If the NDR service does not undertake the matter, or if the amount believed to be in controversy is greater than _____ [same amount], then the parties agree to submit the dispute _____ [e.g., " . . . for *binding* commercial rules arbitration administered by the American Arbitration Association"]. Either party may commence a matter by requesting it in a written demand delivered to the other party and to the administering service stating the subject of the dispute and the relief requested. The place of resolution will be _____ [e.g., online, and/or city or county, and state]. The final resolution and the terms of this paragraph shall be enforceable in any court of competent jurisdiction, and the prevailing party in such enforcement action shall be entitled to recover its reasonable attorney's fees and costs so incurred, along with all of its fees and costs paid to the service administering the agreed resolution process.

The range of possible variation is great. As with more tradition-al ADR methods, many simpler, more comprehensive, or customized constructs of NDR clauses are available. Also, different contract-writing attorneys will prefer different language to address possible ambiguities or concerns.

THE CASE OF THE WEBSITE DESIGN BILL

A small, two-owner/operator website design company contracted with a fast-growing venture-backed data technology company to redesign and upgrade the latter's website and brand messaging. Their written contract was for a total of $100,000 in design and implementation ser-vices to be spread over two phases, with phase one to be completed for $60,000 on an expedited basis in less than three months. The contract also included the right of either party to terminate the contract on 30 days' written notice and an NDR clause governing any disputes.

As the project advanced, the design company suffered unexpect-ed project manager turnover and subcontractor cost overruns, while the tech company became disenchanted with aspects of the design company's performance. The first phase was completed on time, but the tech company decided to terminate the contract at that point. It paid the design company's phase one invoices for $60,000, but refused to pay the company's request for a $12,000 progress payment contem-plated in the contract for preliminary phase two work that the latter already had performed.

The businesspeople on both sides were unable to settle their dif-ferences amicably, so the tech company handed the matter to its out-side legal counsel, a major national and international law firm, to play hardball. Two days later, the tech company withdrew its outstanding settlement offer of $5,000, effectively inviting (or daring) the design company to hire a lawyer to sue for the $12,000. The tech company and its lawyers knew that discovery and other legal costs alone would make any lawsuit a losing proposition for both sides with the burdens of expense, distracted time, and delay falling disproportionately harder on the smaller company. The design company, however, invoked the NDR clause in the contract to engage a mutually acceptable Neutral expert to investigate the dispute quickly, fairly, and inexpensively for both parties.

The NDR provider promptly reached out to both sides' principals and began the search for Neutral candidates. Embarrassed at not having read the contract or investigated all pertinent facts, the tech company's lawyers finally did both. Within a few days, they emailed their client's "one-time offer" in settlement of all issues to pay the design company the full $12,000 asked. The email was written in an aggressive and provocative (face-saving?) style, and the settlement offer was made "on the condition" that the design company would not mention or promote in its marketing that the tech company had been its customer. The lawyers even attached a short settlement agreement that they had drafted. The design company was only too delighted to comply, signed the agreement, and received payment soon after.

The entire resolution process lasted *seven days* from the day the design company invoked the NDR clause to the email capitulation by the tech company. As for cost, the design company incurred *no* legal fees and the tech company paid a small *fraction* of the legal fees it would have spent litigating the case.

TAKEAWAY: WHO DOESN'T LIKE FREE INSURANCE?

Even without the benefit of the above case illustration, you may already have intuited that there are boons from writing NDR clauses into contracts that go well beyond the savings in money, time, relationships, and stress that are gained in actually using the method. And you would be right.

The website design bill case reveals compelling bonuses in specifying NDR in contracts long before any dispute arises: First, very simply, far fewer disappointments and disagreements will turn into legal disputes, and most will settle quickly, as would-be opposing sides and their lawyers quickly realize they have little to gain from making unreasonable claims and threats. Indeed, the built-in disincentive to overly aggressive or fees-motivated lawyering completely realigns attorneys' best interests to coincide with those of their clients, who have a right to expect a fast, reliable, and rational cost solution so that they can get back to doing what they do best. Second, this huge bonus costs *nothing*.

> *Very simply, far fewer disappointments and disagreements will turn into legal disputes, and most will settle quickly, as would-be opposing sides and their lawyers quickly realize they have little to gain from making unreasonable claims and threats.*

Indeed, it's fair to think of NDR in a contract as an effective risk management tool that is a bit like (but not in fact) *free litigation insurance*[3] for deterring meritless or unnecessary disputes. More specifically:

- Advance agreement to use NDR can protect you against *both* Jekyll-turned-Hyde business or trading partners and lawyers who are litigious, extortive, bullying, crazy, greedy, opportunistic, or just plain dishonest—all by reducing their incentives and the ability to threaten, bring, or defend an irrational and expensive lawsuit, while enabling you to obtain justice when necessary at very reasonable cost and investment of time. In short, fewer unreasonable claims (or defenses) will be asserted, and those that *are* should be settled or decided quickly, fairly, and inexpensively.

- Potentially as important, pre-dispute contractual NDR protects you against yourself. If *you* have made a mistake, are responsible for the mistake of an employee or agent, or find yourself falling prey to your own ego or emotional trigger or blind spot, it enables you to face and accept that reality (albeit grudgingly) at *far less* wasteful cost, time, and stress. It may even help you salvage reputation or a relationship because of how you've chosen to manage such situations.

- Finally, even just *proposing* NDR in a contract also has real value, because it conveys your commitment to a win-win relationship and your willingness to take responsibility for any mistakes you may make, and your counterparts' responses will tell you about their character and how they will approach their own mistakes. Indeed, you might suspect that a party to a contract who refuses this approach for smaller disputes either is a high risk to extort or stonewall you if a dispute arises, or is already represented by lawyers unable or unwilling to see the real net advantages for their client in agreeing to NDR.

SIDEBAR

Some naysayers will argue that a determined nut or leverage seeker can always find ways to unfairly threaten and burden the honest and rational among us. Refusals to participate, to comply with decisions, delay, and other legal maneuvers are just a few possibilities. A well-constructed NDR clause, however, undermines the effectiveness of any of these strategies by exposing the noncomplying party to a greater likelihood of an adverse decision and, in any event, the potential obligation to pay for any and all of the other party's additional costs in enforcing the agreed clause.

The only threat that contractual NDR provisions are unlikely to counter effectively is the leverage card held by an "800 lb. gorilla" business or trading partner to discontinue future relations if you don't make undeserved concessions, especially if that ape believes it can do so with impunity. Unfortunately, that is an unavoidable reality of any business dependency, regardless of agreed contract terms. Fortunately, the speed and power of the Internet today to review, expose, and induce changes in ape-like practices, and the growing business wisdom of being perceived as a good business partner, increasingly discourage using unfair leverage.

WHAT DO WE DO WHEN THERE'S NO NDR CONTRACT CLAUSE?

Of course, most limited stakes legal disputes are either between strangers or born of relationships that don't have the benefit of a standing agreement to use NDR. That's one of the systemic reasons we have a civil justice gap. Nevertheless, even in these situations, NDR already has shown real potential for reducing the gap.

The Case of the Crook Who Wasn't

In Indiana, one party had supplied the other with a power supply product for an experimental electric vehicle. A warranty dispute arose. The parties were so polarized that they couldn't talk with one another. Each had come to see the other as a crook who couldn't honestly believe his own arguments. Both were threatening litigation, with only about $12,000 at stake. They had no contract terms covering dispute resolution, so there was no agreement to use NDR or any other ADR process.

The maker of the power supply product contacted a new NDR provider about resolving the parties' differences. The NDR provider explained the process, including its potential net savings and benefits to both parties. The power supply maker committed to the method if the electric vehicle company could be persuaded to do the same. The NDR provider, curious how a "neutral outreach" would be received, contacted the carmaker both by letter and follow-up phone conversations, proposing NDR in lieu of both parties' lawyering up and possibly litigating. A copy of this first initial dispute outreach letter is **Appendix C**.

The NDR provider made full disclosure of the circumstances and let both parties know the consequences of the slippery slope on which they were perched. This compelling combination—mediator-like shuttle diplomacy by telephone, a proposal to use NDR, and the knowledge that both sides were otherwise looking at spending more than the dispute was worth—frankly did little to change each side's perception that the other was misguided and wrong-headed, but it *did convince each* that his counterpart truly believed he was right and was prepared to act on that belief. This critical revelation enabled the two bickering business partners to take fresh looks at each other's positions, reopen a direct dialogue, and settle their differences.

Having proved the efficacy of neutral outreach, the NDR provider subsequently began to offer this service and charge modest fixed fees (from $500 to $1450) depending on size of dispute and estimated work, with that fee to be credited against the requesting party's account if an NDR process resulted. Consequently, paid initial dispute outreaches have taken place in numerous contexts, including shareholder-management, vendor services, potential fraud, real estate sale, insurance coverage, car repair, family club memberships, and other disputes. So far, outreaches tend to result in resumed dialogue and an amicable resolution about 40% of the time—with or without attorneys involved. Also, whether successful or not, the party receiving the outreach inevitably replies to and usually talks with the independent NDR provider, which helps inform the initiating party's future decision-making in any event.

The Cases of the Former Employees

In dealing with occasional threats of limited stakes lawsuits by former employees, an employer's in-house counsel lamented the recurring dilemma of trying to sort phony and extortionate nuisance value threats by opportunists from potentially valid claims that warrant reasonable compensation. Consequently, in multiple dispute negotiations, the employer decided to offer NDR as an alternative to its final offer.

In one case, the former employee asserted she had been wrongfully terminated based on her sexual orientation. Negotiations were on the verge of stalling, as both sides typically proclaimed their clients' confidence in being vindicated in court. *Proposing* NDR, however, instantly led to a breakthrough. The willingness of one side to "let the chips fall where they may" in an indisputably and mutually fair and affordable process led by an independent investigator and adjudicator signaled real strength, honest belief, and a genuine commitment to fairness. That immediately tested the other side's *bona fides*. Acceptance, like the proposal itself, would prompt both parties to take fresh looks at their strengths and weaknesses. Rejection, on the other hand, could suggest weakness on the merits—that is, who should win—and/or a desire to extort money by leveraging factors such as the employer's likely costs of defense. In short, either reply would deliver valuable intelligence to guide next moves. In this instance, the employee declined NDR, but immediately elected to accept the employer's prior best (and very low) cash offer.

In another case, the former employee claimed he had been set up to fail at his job and wrongfully terminated in retaliation for complaining that his supervisors were biased against him due to his national origin. The dispute was governed by an agreement to arbitrate. When early negotiations bogged down, the employer's general counsel offered NDR to settle the case, and the employee and his counsel agreed. The parties then agreed on the Neutral, a fixed fee for the process (to be paid by the employer in lieu of arbitration fees), and a range within which any damages award must fall. Both sides viewed the other's willingness to agree to NDR as an honest belief that they were right and would be vindicated by the Neutral's decision. Because of this, and knowing the amount of the fixed Neutral's fee for conducting the NDR process, the parties quickly negotiated a settlement acceptable to both.

> *In an employment dispute, both sides viewed the other's willingness to agree to NDR as an honest belief that they were right and would be vindicated by the Neutral's decision. Because of this, and knowing the amount of the fixed Neutral's fee for conducting the NDR process, the parties quickly negotiated a settlement acceptable to both.*

In each of the above cases, *both* sides probably secured much better and more satisfying *net results* than they would have through litigation, and both exited with honor intact. Since then, the in-house counsel has continued to propose NDR to break impasses and quickly lead to fast and inexpensive resolutions for the employer and acceptable net settlements for former employees before the cases could blow up out of control. The employer also now includes NDR as a voluntary grievance resolution option in its employee handbook, and encourages its HR department to offer NDR whenever the resolution of an employee dispute may benefit from an independent neutral intervention.

The Case of the Frustrated Shareholders

An investor group in California became concerned that the once-promising biomedical start-up in which its members had invested was not being managed well or honestly. Specifically, they feared that the CEO was not assigning important patents to the company and possibly was engaging in other self-dealing in connection with negotiations to sell the company. The investors did not wish to disrupt the all-important sale negotiations, but they felt their representative on the Board of Directors had been shut out of communications and denied access concerning the status of the company and potential sale in breach of their shareholder agreements.

Had they retained counsel to threaten litigation, doing so very possibly could have resulted in unwanted compelled disclosure to prospective buyers, and would have triggered spending precious investment capital on legal fees by both sides. Instead, the investor group retained an NDR provider as a neutral facilitator to get the attention of the company and CEO, obtain the communications and information to which the investors' designated director was entitled, and, if necessary, help the parties find a mutually acceptable Neutral to sort out differences privately.

The neutral facilitator commenced this "Initial Dispute Outreach" by letter. The CEO and outside company counsel refused to submit to NDR, but encouraged continued dialogue through the NDR facilitator, paid by the investor group. Several telephone calls and meetings ensued among the NDR facilitator, the investor group, company counsel, and company officers, concluding with the investor group's director gaining satisfactory access to the information sought, confirmation that all patents were assigned to the company, and the successful sale of the company a few months later. Each side expended less than $5,000 in professional fees to resolve the parties' differences effectively and quietly and enable the later sale at a value of many millions of dollars.

Takeaway: The Power of Suggestion

Just *proposing* NDR at the beginning of a dispute, whether via neutral outreach by an NDR provider or in direct negotiations with an opposing party, has very real value—if not a compelling role to play—in resolving almost any limited stakes dispute. In the case of neutral outreach by an NDR provider, there may be some cost associated because it requires an investment of real time and skill, but that cost should be low given that the NDR provider has an incentive to succeed via the opportunity to administer the NDR process.

My recommended version of a compensated neutral outreach works like this:

- The first party contacts the NDR provider, identifies the parties, nature, and size of the dispute, and declares a willingness to resolve the dispute via NDR.

- The first party retains the NDR provider *as a neutral facilitator* to reach out to the second party for a small, fixed fee that will be fully credited toward the first party's share of any subsequent NDR process fees.

- The NDR provider sends the second party an introductory letter identifying its retention in a neutral capacity, the general subject and nature of the apparent dispute, the costs and risks if the dispute takes the adversarial path to resolution, and the gains and savings to both sides if they choose NDR instead.

- The NDR provider follows up with both parties until one of three things happens: they contractually agree to an NDR process for the specific dispute in question, they resume direct negotiations and agree to a dollar-specific settlement, or one party definitively rejects NDR.

Until NDR is better known, understood, and accepted as a viable and effective tool for bridging the civil justice gap, getting parties to agree to it *after* a dispute has arisen will be an uphill battle. Once a dispute arises and becomes intractable, distrust and suspicion of *any* initiative or idea from "the other side" is usually too great to overcome. Nevertheless, just as in pre-dispute contracting, I contend—and the case studies seem to support—that there is real value in proposing NDR in many conflict negotiations, because:

- Many fine lawyers and businesspeople *are* enlightened, *do* believe in the rightness of their cause, are *not* trying to game the system or satisfy greed, and so may entertain and welcome the mutual gains and savings for the parties. If one side is looking for a way to stand on principle in a limited stakes dispute without having to foolishly risk more than the dispute is worth, they can propose NDR. If the other side accepts, regardless of who wins, both are likely to invest far less time and stress, and wind up better off financially and reputationally than if they had litigated.

- As a negotiating tool, proposing NDR conveys an unambiguous message of honest strength and confidence in the merits of one's position. There is nothing weak or subject to misinterpretation about a willingness to bet on oneself and accept the consequences. This is often quite surprising to and unexpected by the other party, who often has already demonized their opponent. Consequently, it forces the other party (and counsel) to closely examine the merits of their position. This can lead to reassessment and rekindled negotiations, desirable dissention between opposing counsel and client if one of them is not thinking straight, or even retreat and capitulation to the last best offer or demand made. Finally, if the other party refuses, the proposal may lay bare the lie in that party's professed absolute confidence in the merits of its position, for who would *not* choose a process leading to vindication at a fraction of the cost and invested time? In any event, you will gain insight into what to expect from this party as an opponent.

- Proposing NDR takes the moral high ground. It says that you're committed to fair dealing even in the face of strong disagreement.

- There's little to lose in suggesting it.

CHAPTER SUMMARY

- NDR not only makes sense in concept, it truly works in actual practice. Several real-life stories illustrate different uses of NDR in winning genuine justice.

- When a contractor sued its customer for $28,000 in expenses for undue delay, it took only a few weeks and less than $1,500 per side to have a mutually chosen arbiter investigate and correctly decide the dispute, thanks to the parties already having a contractual dispute resolution clause specifying NDR. By comparison, a similar $30,000 dispute that was litigated instead cost *each* side over $30,000 in legal fees before settling on the eve of trial.

- A venture-backed technology company hired a major law firm to stonewall a $12,000 progress payment owed to a small website design company, until the latter invoked the NDR clause already in their contract. Within a week, the dispute settled for the full amount claimed.

- Contract clauses specifying NDR can be as simple or as complex as the parties require. This is illustrated by two sample clauses: a short basic one, and a two-tiered clause that sends smaller disputes to NDR and larger ones to arbitration.

- A warranty dispute arose between small companies working in the then-experimental electric vehicle industry. No contract terms covered dispute resolution, but one side contacted an NDR provider who then *neutrally* reached out to the other. When faced with the likely costs of litigating and recognition that the "other guy" also honestly believed he was right, both sides were persuaded to start talking again and quickly resolved their differences amicably. The initial dispute outreach letter from this dispute is **Appendix C**.

- During stalled negotiations in an employment discrimination dispute, the employer's general counsel proposed NDR to the plaintiff's attorney. The willingness of one side to "let the chips fall where they may" in a plainly fair, independent, and affordable process communicated real strength and genuine belief that the other side failed to match, triggering an immediate breakthrough and very low settlement based on a previous offer. By contrast, in a similar dispute, the same employer and another former employee *agreed* to NDR. The parties retained an expert Neutral who quoted a reasonable fixed fee to investigate and decide the dispute. This cooperation and belief on both sides led to a fair settlement just before the NDR got underway.

- Corporate shareholders proposed NDR to successfully persuade management to honor their information rights without jeopardizing a sale of the company.

- Even where there's no contractual NDR contract clause, proposing this method to resolve a dispute is a powerful negotiating tool that invites the other side to either share the moral high ground (and reduce everyone's costs) or reveal a weak stance.

www.CartoonStock.com

"A lawyer unpaid is justice denied."

CHAPTER 9

CHALLENGES TO ADOPTION

If NDR works so well and makes such a difference, why isn't it like Starbucks—everywhere? Why haven't I heard of it? Why hasn't someone I know suggested it to me?

The easy and grossly unfair answer is simple: Lawyers don't want it and nonlawyers don't know they need it. Like most complex equations, the true reasons are interdependent, more nuanced, and,

143

of course, subject to exceptions. Together, these reasons pose real challenges to broad adoption and widespread use of NDR by clients and lawyers alike—no matter how much better it is for everyone in the many situations where it does make sense. You can guess some of these challenges. Others will surprise you. Since shining a bright light on all is the best first step to overcoming them, I do that here.

CHALLENGE 1

ECONOMICS—THERE'S LITTLE MONEY IN IT FOR DUELING LAWYERS

Put in the plainest words possible, NDR is very good for our clients, but appears not to be so good for litigation attorneys. NDR—both as process and as negotiating tool—slashes legal fees earnable in potential and actual disputes where it's invoked. In the case of almost all limited stakes disputes, this happens in a way that typically improves the net quality, quantity, speed, and procurement costs of justice *for all parties*. Similarly, NDR appears to lower the fees earned by third-party neutral services who make their money administering litigator-driven mediations and arbitrations, as their business models rely on and target litigation attorneys as their primary customers. Finally, this lower fees equation appears to apply even to third-party NDR providers, since merely invoking NDR is so effective at reopening settlement dialogue and enabling a fair and prompt settlement that few disputes subject to it need actually proceed through the whole process.

In short, NDR's benefit to clients of greatly reduced net legal costs offers little immediate economic incentive to litigators and third-party neutral services to learn, recommend, or use this tool, and may even incite passive resistance and active skepticism.

IS THIS A MOUNTAIN OF LOSS
OR A MOLE HILL OF PARANOIA?

The real shame of the above economic disincentive is that in practice it's much smaller than otherwise may appear. Here's why:

First, since most limited stakes cases in fact *settle* during early negotiations (often *because* of the threat that legal fees will consume the stakes), attorneys who've been hired to advise clients of their rights, options, and best strategies, and to negotiate and document these settlements, *will in fact lose little or no legal fees to NDR*. They'll continue to play the same gatekeeper/advisor/strategist/negotiator role in most situations—no matter what forums are available or specified—and 90% or more of cases will still settle (some of them via NDR).💡

BRIEF

One might wonder if NDR occasionally could have the unintended consequence of promoting more disputes and delaying some settlements. After all, agreeing to NDR removes the threat of high legal fees as settlement leverage in negotiations. The prospect of faster, cheaper justice might embolden parties to seek vindication more often. Even if this *were* to happen, it hardly seems undesirable. In all events, these occasions should be few and more than offset by the net reduction in litigation that NDR delivers.

Second, few litigation attorneys rely on legal fees from limited stakes cases for their livelihoods. Almost all spend most of their time (and make the lion's share of their money) on more complex, high stakes matters that justify all the effort and skill they can bring to bear in order to obtain the best outcomes possible for their clients. These attorneys, too, will lose little in the way of fees to NDR.

Third, many attorneys routinely welcome early practical settlements *in smaller cases*, because these cases otherwise create pressure to substantially discount their fees. They know that early practical settlements enable them to take on or turn to more lucrative fee-earning matters, while earning and preserving the loyalty of clients who otherwise would have good reason to regret their experience and possibly blame their counsel. Indeed, that same goodwill and loyalty may even be earned in pay-it-forward fashion whenever an attorney is able to refer an otherwise "nobody-wins-but-the-lawyers" case to NDR.

Fourth, there's another powerful economic reality that mitigates the potential net impact of NDR on lawyers' opportunities to earn legal fees: Most lawsuits are *not* between parties to contracts who've agreed to NDR in advance, and, as a practical matter, *it takes only one* party *or* lawyer in such a lawsuit to refuse NDR and force all to travel the traditional path. Consequently, most limited stakes disputes will continue to be resolved without the many benefits of NDR for years to come.

Fifth, there are plenty of off-setting *fee-earning* opportunities for lawyers *within* NDR. Lawyers can choose to serve as NDR Neutrals (just as many attorneys serve as mediators and arbitrators), advise or speak for their clients *during* the NDR process, write and negotiate NDR provisions into contracts, and propose NDR in settlement negotiations. Similarly, neutral ADR service providers who add NDR to their mediation and arbitration offerings should earn off-setting fees in administering NDR cases, because NDR Neutrals play a larger, proactive investigator role.

BRIEF

Nevertheless, I believe that traditional third-party ADR services will be slow to include NDR as an option until it is in greater use, as these services will be concerned about the risk of offending their primary market (lawyers) and cannibalizing their business model (selling to lawyers).

LAWYER TRAINING AND PROFESSIONAL STANDARDS—NDR IS OUTSIDE THE BOX

Law school and early professional training teach law and legal skills. This means that, with few exceptions, neither formal nor on-the-job training teaches young lawyers how to save clients' time, money, and frustration. Nor do they teach about the insidious hidden costs of litigation and how to estimate those costs to help clients make more informed decisions. Law schools also don't give practical instruction in balancing the costs and value of vigorous advocacy in light of what's at stake, and in creating and using nontraditional and innovative alternatives that would more effectively make justice accessible at truly reasonable cost. While law school and early career training now teach *lawyer*-driven ADR like arbitration and mediation, they don't usually teach *neutral*-driven solutions like NDR. Instead, lawyer training in problem-solving is limited to tools inside the box of law, legal process, and advocacy—tools that, not coincidentally, only lawyers may wield.

These gaps in young lawyer training are hardly accidental. State regulation and rules governing professional legal practice and ethics define and require lawyer **competence** only in terms of traditional legal training and tools,[1] and too often provide little direction or incentive for them to inform clients of reasonable and alternative outside-the-box paths that could achieve client goals while saving time, money, and frustration.

BRIEF

While all state rules require lawyers to obtain their clients' **informed consent** to a proposed course of conduct, some require only that the lawyer explain the plan's **relevant circumstances** and **material risks** (e.g., California Rules of Professional Conduct 1.4(a)(b) and 1.0.1). This common "legalese" lacks any plain and clear mandate to identify and compare different available courses of conduct or explain the advantages and disadvantages of each to the client. (California Rule 2.1 does *allow* lawyers to consider moral, economic, social, and political factors that may be relevant to a client's situation, but the California rules pointedly and explicitly do not *require* these considerations.) While I have not undertaken a comprehensive survey of all state variations on this critical rule, at least one, Maine, laudably stands out as stating the rule of *informed* client consent in plain language: Maine Rule of Professional Conduct 1.0 adopts a Model (i.e., recommended) Rule from the American Bar Association requiring that attorneys inform clients about "reasonably available alternatives" to whatever they propose, and then explain "the *advantages and risks* involved, . . . and *any other circumstances* bearing on whether the client has made a reasoned and deliberate choice [emphasis added]."

Given lawyers' gatekeeper role in legal matters and our culture's traditional reliance on their advice, deficiencies in legal training and professional standards are among the most powerful influences preventing our recognition and adoption of a better path for many limited stakes disputes. Admittedly, these omissions have little consequence in small claims cases—where lawyers are limited to advisory roles—and in high stakes cases—where full-blown competitive advocacy is likely to be worth its many costs. However, they have immense consequences in those many disputes that fall between, where they limit *all* lawyers' perceptions of the tools available to help their clients and leave many lawyers distrustful, defensive, and skeptical about unfamiliar innovative paths.

To this extent, lawyers can hardly be faulted for relying upon the narrow tools in which they have been trained—even if those tools may not serve their clients' overall best interests. Lawyers, especially those representing businesses, are notoriously conservative about real innovation in legal practice, and are naturally very skeptical of any change that challenges their central role in solving their clients' legal problems. Some of that conservatism and skepticism is justified by their state-mandated duties and risk aversion to possible professional malpractice claims. In any event, until they have personal experience or reliable reported experience of an effective new approach (even one that stands to benefit their clients, themselves, and the reputation of the profession), they will be slow to adopt real and meaningful innovation while there is safety in sticking with traditional tools. In sum, law school curricula and continuing legal education need to be broadened to encompass NDR, and state ethical rules ought to be reviewed and revised to encourage (if not require) all attorneys to bring a broader, more truly client-centric, and economically sensitive perspective to legal representation—at least in limited stakes disputes.

CHALLENGE 3

LAWYER EGOS—GETTING OUT OF THE WAY IS HARD TO SEE, HARDER TO DO

Are lawyers willing to get out of the way when it helps their clients? You may be surprised that I believe the answer is yes for most lawyers. I've worked with, against, and around many hundreds of lawyers. I've found the vast majority of them to be conscientious people who are devoted to serving their clients' best interests. Even among my opponents, only a small percentage of these hundreds have proved to be chronic liars or more interested in their fees than in their clients' well-being.

Regardless of personal style, most of us lawyers—myself included—have big egos. This is especially true of litigators. We almost *have* to think well of ourselves in order to do what we do—which is spend our professional lives dealing with mostly smart, determined opponents and frustrated, unhappy, and sometimes angry clients.

For all our good intentions, these big egos can sometimes blind us to the best ways of helping our clients. Two common blind spots in particular play a large, subconscious role in attorneys re-sisting client-helping innovations like NDR. These are the myth of control and the "not invented here" (NIH) syndrome.

OVERCOMING THE MYTH OF CONTROL

When it comes to dispute resolution, the parties and their lawyers often believe the longer they can maintain control of their fates, the better and more satisfying a result they'll earn, and the less it will cost overall. Lawyers are especially susceptible to this perception, partic-ularly early in a dispute. It's usually *not* because we know that we'll earn more fees the longer the dispute lasts (although we will), or that we're hoping to cultivate and exploit the disputing parties' anger and frustration with each other (although I've seen it done). Most of us are really *not* greedy and conniving—popular sentiment notwithstanding.

For most lawyers, there are two reasons for maintaining control that delays resolution. First, we don't know enough. The beginning of a case is when we know the least about the dispute—what happened, what our client hasn't told us or doesn't know, what the opposing party actually believes and thinks, what claims, defenses, and law may prove to be the most important, the competence of the other side's lawyer, and what strategies and tactics may maximize our client's prospects for achieving the best realistic outcome possible. Second, we don't want to risk a poor settlement. We don't want to risk committing malpractice or some other mistake by prematurely offering or accepting a worse outcome for our client than necessary. So we believe it makes sense to delay settlement until we can learn enough and reduce our risks to the point that we're reasonably sure we're getting the best possible deal for our client.

In limited stakes disputes, however, nothing could be further from the truth.

Let's recall from Chapter 1 that the outcomes of limited stakes disputes are determined, probably well over 90% of the time, by what actually happened and what law applies (plus occasional uncontrollable variables)—and not by anything competent lawyers do or don't do. Yes, the contest *can* become like a poker game where each side tests the other side's card hand, looks for "tells," or bluffs through rounds of ever-increasing bets (usually with the client's money). However, the analogy breaks down, because in litigation each side gets to see the other's "hand" before trial (via investigation and discovery), so the odds very strongly favor that the better hand will be revealed and ultimately win.

In Chapter 5, we also discussed that individual parties and their lawyers in fact *never really have control over how disputes end.* By definition, settling a case requires the consent of the other side, and proceeding to trial and judgment entails a decision by an authorized third party. Moreover, it's not just that lawyers and their clients can't and don't actually control litigation. Litigation in fact controls *them.*

This is easy to see by recognizing that real control is a myth. The only thing each side can control is its own acts, which quickly cause, as in Newton's Third Law of Motion, at least equal and opposite reactions, or even unpredictable escalation triggered by ego and emotional response in lawyer and client alike. It's as if the parties share a staircase going up to an uncertain level above. Each time one takes a step to catch up or pass, the other feels compelled to do likewise. In either case—reaction or overreaction—we know that in limited stakes disputes *every act* and *every week* that passes after initial settlement negotiations break down increases *every* party's total costs of litigation in money, distracted time and energy, stress, and unsalvageable relationships. This rapidly consumes any chance of a net outcome for *either* side that satisfactorily resolves the dispute at total costs lower than what's at stake. Eventually, when the legal bills and other costs become high enough, one or both sides usually recognize the insanity of the journey and settle for the smallest net loss they can, but by then the damage has been done. *When the stakes are limited, delaying resolution simply means parties spend more to get less.*

FORTUNATELY, THE SITUATION ISN'T HOPELESS

If there's no effective way for lawyers to overcome the unknowns that can delay early settlement, then they'll cling to whatever control they think they have. Fortunately, NDR is a tool that can solve their dilemma. NDR *is* an early settlement agreement, not to a sum of money, but to a fast, fair, truth-focused, less stressful, and far cheaper *process* and outcome with little opportunity for ego-driven delay or escalation. Consequently, it relieves both sides of any need to speculate about or suffer a fate based on mistakes due to woefully inadequate information. Certainly in NDR, just as in court, arbitration, or mediation, there are risks of error or ultimate injustice, but NDR's risks are no greater. Indeed, because NDR removes the element of gamesmanship, those risks may well be lower than in other processes, while the real gains to clients are substantial.

> *NDR* is *an early settlement agreement, not to a sum of money, but to a fast, fair, truth-focused, less stressful, and far cheaper* process *and outcome with little opportunity for ego-driven delay or escalation.*

NOT INVENTED HERE: THE PRICE
OF KNEE-JERK DISTRUST

The "not invented here" (NIH) syndrome is at least as common among lawyers as the myth of control. This is a subconscious tendency or attitude to resist good ideas or innovations that are not one's own.[2] Behavioral psychologists perceive this syndrome as part of an attitude of resentment of others' skills and talents and a preference for only doing things that one already does well. It consequently is a general barrier to maximum learning and better outcomes, afflicting those who have "fixed" or "closed" mindsets (as opposed to persons with "growth" or "open" mindsets who consistently seek out, are inspired by, and freely credit best ideas regardless of source). Whatever label we give it, as an ego-driven obstacle to NDR, the "not invented here" syndrome is immense.

-☀- **BRIEF** _____

The works of psychologists Carol S. Dweck, PhD, Eve Grodnitzky, PhD, and Adam Grant, PhD, reflect leading-edge thinking and helpful prescriptions in this field.[3]

_____

The problem begins with the fact that a number of people, including many lawyers, are disinclined to look favorably on and accept good ideas or solutions from others. It stands to reason that if one is fully open to evaluating others' ideas objectively, that person will tend to make better, more rational decisions, and generally be a more effective learner and leader.

In everyday business and personal relations, the NIH syndrome is a common roadblock to better judgments and solutions of every kind. Smart businesses and other organizations now study this obstacle and take steps to prevent it from hijacking important brainstorming and problem-solving action plans.[4] In the field of dispute resolution, distrust of the motives of opposing attorneys and their clients naturally runs very high and training in negotiation techniques often calls for brinksmanship requiring rejection and counteroffer to *whatever* the other side proposes. The negative impact is devastating.

This happens so often that I cannot begin to tell you how many failed opportunities for *early, fair, and economically rational* dispute resolutions I've encountered in my career because of one side's automatic, knee-jerk assumption and reaction that anything which their *enemy* would suggest either can't be good for them or can't be the other side's real bottom line. This is just as true whether the proposal on the table is for a specific payment of money as it is for a fair and mutually economical alternative process.

Of course, there often are legitimate reasons to reject an opponent's fair proposal. Inadequate knowledge, as discussed in the last section, can be one. Perceived tactical or strategic advantage is another. There are also many not-so-legitimate reasons, including delay for delay's sake, self-serving convenience, face-saving posturing with clients, and poor factual or legal analysis. But all too often the evidence points simply to the ego-driven fact that because *the other side* made the proposal, it was automatically treated with suspicion, envy, or both, and then rejected without any objective analysis. To the extent that this syndrome is alive and well in current dispute negotiations, and given the practical reality that it only takes one person among any two lawyers and two clients to block agreement, NIH is a major obstacle to NDR that will be difficult to overcome in many instances.

Moreover, the NIH syndrome is a form of subconscious bias, and, like most forms of bias, the afflicted cannot recognize it in themselves. Consequently, there is no ready answer other than for persons not so afflicted to think for themselves, question for understanding, and bravely decide (as the client) or advise (as the lawyer) in favor of good ideas and solutions—regardless of who suggested them first.

SIDEBAR

It's Not Always the Lawyer

In 2018, a married couple signed a written contract to buy a home in San Jose, California, subject to the condition that the city approve their plans to improve the property. They deposited $36,000 into escrow with the seller/owner and proceeded to incur about $24,000 in professional, engineering, architectural, and other fees and costs.

The city initially refused to approve the plans within the time the parties had expected. The buyers claimed the seller/owner had verbally agreed to extend the closing date and they had relied on this commitment, but the seller denied doing so. He also argued that the city's rejection of the plans was the fault of the buyers and their architect, who were unfamiliar with city regulations. The parties accused each other of breach of contract and the buyers demanded the return of their $60,000 investment.

Both parties hired lawyers. Legal claims and cross claims were filed. The judge ordered the case to nonbinding arbitration before setting it for trial, a common practice in California and many courts. The lawyers found a mutually acceptable arbitrator. They were very concerned that both sides were about to waste far more money on a nonbinding process than the case was worth. Even if they agreed to make the arbitration binding, both parties would still spend most or all that was at stake in legal and arbitration process fees.

One of those lawyers was a colleague who knew that I promoted use of NDR, so he suggested this to the other side. Because both lawyers already shared the view that arbitration could be a waste of time and money, they were both open to the idea and without much difficulty convinced their clients to agree to NDR. The already-chosen arbitrator readily agreed to the change in his role and to a modest flat fee of $6,000 per party—about 1/10 of the amount in dispute for each—to proactively investigate, research, analyze, and decide the case. The lawyers stepped back and advised their clients from the sideline.

My fledgling NDR operation acted as administrator, preparing and vetting a simple, mutually acceptable three-way contract. The arbitrator signed. Both lawyers signed. My colleague's clients signed. But the other side's client, the seller/owner, suddenly changed his mind and refused to sign—without explanation or any reason his attorney could share beyond hinting that his client no longer believed NDR was a good enough solution. The seller, although satisfied with the choice of Neutral, apparently became fearful that whatever was proposed by and acceptable to his opponent must be disadvantageous to him.

Since "it only takes one" to nix a sane process and outcome, there was nothing to do but revert to the court's order for nonbinding arbitration. The buyers, while disappointed, were encouraged in their view of the case by their opponent's rejection of a plainly fair and inexpensive process, so they refused the discounted compromise next offered by the seller. The case then proceeded toward arbitration to include depositions, briefs, counter-briefs, a trial-like hearing with witness testimony and documents, a nonbinding decision, and likely subsequent threats by whoever lost to proceed to trial—all at a likely total further cost to each side of $30,000 to $60,000 in legal, arbitrator, and trial fees.

A few weeks later, the seller suddenly and completely folded his hand and agreed to return the buyers' money. Whether he was bluffing all along is unknown. The buyers' lawyer later told me he believed this was a good outcome for NDR because it forced the parties to get real very quickly.

CHALLENGE 4

UNFAMILIARITY—NDR LACKS VISIBILITY AND TOP-OF-MIND AWARENESS

Visibility, including "Top-of-Mind Awareness" (TOMA), is a fundamental marketing concept. All products and services need to be visible to potential customers or other end users in order to be considered for purchase or use. Businesses universally also want TOMA, because it means their product or service comes to mind first or immediately when customers or potential customers have need for or think about that category of product or service.[5] In the category of services known as ADR (alternative dispute resolution), it's fair to say that after decades of development and use, arbitration and mediation enjoy both visibility and TOMA—with lawyers and most clients. Despite its promise, NDR at present lacks these attributes—another key reason why it's not yet in widespread use in situations where it can do great good.

As you might guess, the first three challenges discussed above—lawyer economics, training, and egos—variously contribute to NDR's challenge of being the new kid on the block. The combination of little fee-earning opportunity, myopic training, and big egos are enough in their own right to slow awareness and adoption. However, add to them a general lack of familiarity in the marketplace and an already formidable barrier becomes monstrous.

NEVER HEARD OF NDR

NDR is new. It's different. It works a bit like both arbitration and mediation (but without key drawbacks of either), such that nonlawyers seldom understand it at first glance. 💡

BRIEF

"How is NDR different from mediation or arbitration?" is the first question I get from almost every nonlawyer with whom I speak about it. The fundamental difference is easy to say and grasp: The *Neutral* investigates the facts and law in NDR, while *opposing attorneys* do that in mediation and arbitration. However, that single difference ultimately leads to multiple *costs savings* and other beneficial *impacts* in terms of time, money, relationships, and stress that defy quick description and recognition.

Unfortunately, that first glance is often the only time and attention a new product or service can garner in the age of Internet marketing and advertising. So much is constantly thrown at us now that we have become conditioned to ignore or dismiss anything that doesn't immediately confirm what we already believe. Moreover, while NDR primarily benefits *clients*, it's *lawyers* on whom clients depend as gatekeepers to all things legal in a world of increasing complexity, specialization, and overall "speed" of life. We already know why many lawyers might not know about or propose using NDR. Effectively educating the user marketplace about NDR thus becomes a tall and difficult order.

I've been singing the praises of NDR—promoting it, recommending it, and using it in my own legal practice whenever possible—for more than a decade. My first website promoting the method posted about 2006 while I was still refining details and continuing to practice litigation. I didn't even call it "NDR" then. For lack of a better term, I referred to the process as a "resolve," and I remember posting early promotional emails and ads trying to differentiate it as "the Un-ADR." (For those of you over 50, this was inspired by the famous breakthrough ad campaign for 7-Up, "the Un-Cola," which ran from 1968 until 1998 and tapped into a broad antiestablishment and youthful counterculture sentiment that sought to change the world for the better.)[6]

To some extent, the slow pace of inclusion and adoption of NDR to date is my own fault. I initially believed that already-known and growing neutral-driven processes like **Dispute Resolution Boards** in big construction projects would help me quickly build a critical mass of awareness for and adoption of NDR. I also knew, however, that other contemporary neutral-driven dispute resolution tools have been variously employed for many years without emerging into common practice in the United States today. One such tool is the **Ombudsman**, an official or quasi-public authority appointed in many other countries and numerous universities of the world to impartially investigate public maladministration or violations of civil rights.[7] Another is **Neutral Fact-Finding**, in which a mutually agreed expert investigates and may decide key fact issues chosen by opposing attorneys or a judge in the course of American litigation in order to aid in settling or judging cases.[8]

Because these other neutral-driven tools had never been fully developed, refined, or championed for broad use as an alternative to civil court in the United States, I decided to introduce NDR to the world with care and caution. I also knew that lawyers-turned mediators and arbitrators could not be expected to bite the hands that feed them by developing or leading a charge against the entrenched establishment that hires their services. 💡

 **BRIEF** _____

It almost seems that only a senior insider—someone near retirement, financially independent, deeply disturbed by the waste, having a lifelong outsider's perspective, thick-skinned, and driven by a foolish passion to make a difference for good— would be in a position to study the problem and innovate a better solution that blows the whistle on his profession's hidebound traditions and best-kept secrets. If only we could find such an idiot . . . .

Therefore, taking a page from numerous start-up venture experts, and knowing my industry and profession reasonably well, I chose from the beginning to start small, prove the NDR concept and its effectiveness beyond any doubt, then refine it from lessons learned so that it would work well and reliably in practice. Just as importantly, it needed to survive potential dismissal and naysay from others before ever having a chance to succeed. I also had in mind the important lesson of Sony's Betamax failure against the inferior VHS format in the early market for home video recorders:[9] *The best new solution to an important need doesn't always win out over clever, entrenched, and economically powerful competition.*

I launched NDR relatively quietly—with a simple website, a sequence of earnest marketing consultants, an informal advisory board of local CEOs, and my personal network—in order to build and learn from early experience. I also created a company to deliver the service, because both the NDR method and traditional ADR methods appeared to work best using an independent administrator. That was my test or "beta" plan.

From day one, I encountered all of the challenges noted here. Opposition to real innovation in resolving legal disputes came into play almost immediately, even as I tried to find early experimenters and adopters. Consequently, success came slowly, and monetization of the business model not at all. But through experimentation and refinement, adoption is finally getting traction among numerous brave early-adopter customers—if only at the rate of one contract, company, or case at a time.

A BAD CASE OF ADD

People have a lot to do. So do businesses. And governments. And litigation attorneys. And corporate and other business legal counsel. We all have to prioritize, and putting out fires always moves to the top of the to-do list. Lawsuits are fires that have to be fought now. They can't wait for quiet moments of reflection.

By contrast, *preventing* lawsuits via proactive innovations like NDR lies at the unattended bottom of the priority list. Prevention also requires a would-be adopter to recognize a risk or problem, evaluate its size, scope, and solution, and courageously take both the initiative to act and the risk in so doing. That's a lot of inertia to overcome, especially when clients are unlikely to be faulted for sticking with familiar paths and the advice of those who advocate those paths. Moreover, legal disputes are relatively infrequent events in the lives of most people and organizations, which also contributes to the tendency to ignore their risks until it's too late.

The low priority we give to risks of possible future lawsuits works out well for certain people and organizations, including many lawyers and law firms, whose livelihoods depend on bringing or defending lawsuits. Unfortunately, among these are many opportunists who take advantage of the general population's lack of proactive prevention in order to bring unnecessary or even frivolous lawsuits, to assert weak or frivolous defenses, and ultimately to extort either unjustified tributes of money or the surrender of valid rights in settlement.

At some point in time, almost every person or business seems to fall prey to these opportunists. Parties who've done no wrong or who've made a small and unintended mistake too often pay *far too much* or must accept *far too little*, because they or their counsel learn the costs and risks of asserting their rights will be too great. Perhaps through better understanding of the nature and effectiveness of NDR among honest lawyers and nonlawyers alike, and the knowledge that this method can be specified in contracts before disputes ever arise, NDR will rise to a high enough place in our priorities that we'll learn to act before trouble strikes and thus alleviate future suffering and waste.

> *Perhaps through better understanding of the nature and effectiveness of NDR among honest lawyers and nonlawyers alike, and the knowledge that this method can be specified in contracts before disputes ever arise, NDR will rise to a high enough place in our priorities that we'll learn to act before trouble strikes and thus alleviate future suffering and waste.*

THE CHICKEN AND THE EGG OF TRUST

To some degree, every innovation must address The Chicken and The Egg trust challenge: Which must come first, trust or experience? Without experiencing a new way of doing things, how can I trust it? Without trust, how do I bring myself to even try something new, especially if that something seems to carry risk of loss or embarrassment? NDR, being an innovation with which few have any experience, plainly faces this challenge.

People smarter than I have studied this obstacle and suggested methods to overcome it,[10] beginning with an understanding of the critical role of trust. In his compelling book *The Speed of Trust*, Stephen M. R. Covey eloquently uses real-world illustrations to convey the value of trust in the business world. Without it, he writes, we add great cost to each and every transaction. With it, transaction costs shrink to a small fraction by comparison. When we increase the speed of trust, for example, we don't spend nearly as much time and money agonizing over and evaluating promises or negotiating the minutia of complex contract terms. Covey writes that by the time Warren Buffett decides to buy a company, he's learned so much about the quality, integrity, and core values of the people who own and run it that he knows a handshake deal will lead to the swift completion of final contracts.[11]

Trust is best rooted in experience, of course, but when direct experience is not available—for example, when something is innovative and new—other evidence can open the door to trust or firmly close it.[12] What evidence can an innovative new product or service like NDR deliver to earn enough initial trust for people to try it? Experts suggest there are six kinds of such evidence:

- **Reputation**—whether one's own in a related service, or borrowed from others via their endorsement

- **Commitment**—making and keeping small, clear, meaningful promises in addition to those which are at the core of the basic value proposition

- **Consistency**—this applies to messaging content, as well as to look and feel

- **Transparency**—disdaining secrets to share knowledge openly and honestly

- **Vulnerability**—sharing imperfections, being open to criticism, and fixing mistakes ("People will always trust imperfection with integrity over a perfect façade."[13])

- **Listening**—hearing with the intent to understand and learn

To succeed, NDR will need to avail itself of as many of these kinds of evidence of trustworthiness as possible. 💡

BRIEF

Cultivating a trustworthy reputation *before* many have used NDR requires borrowing from highly respected endorsers in related fields and motivated early adopters who are not afraid to recognize the problem and act on it. My reputation as an effective and caring attorney is not nearly broad enough nor great enough to carry something as big as NDR on its shoulders alone.

Valuable commitments, on the other hand, are something that anyone who provides or promotes NDR ought to be able to deliver now. NDR neutral service providers can commit to no risk/no cost introductory consultations about the merits and effectiveness of NDR. They can also commit to very low flat fees for helping customers either implement NDR in contracts or reach out to opponents when disputes arise, and perhaps to reimburse early adopters to cover the cost to convert NDR decisions into enforceable judgments when needed.

This and other valuable services could be paid for by either a blanket low annual subscription fee or a one-time add-on charge at the outset of specific NDR services. As more and more courts (and legislatures) recognize the process and the good it does, the need for such fees should dissipate. In any event, for the time being, provider commitments could meaningfully reduce customer uncertainty and anxiety enough to give NDR a chance.

CHALLENGE 5

CULTURE—WE HAVE MET THE ENEMY AND IT IS US

Unlike the challenges described so far, it's primarily we as clients—as *users* and *consumers* of legal services—who bear primary responsibility for the cultural challenge to innovations like NDR. As observed in Chapter 4, our American legal system is a reflection of who we are—a freedom-loving people of fierce independence and elevated individualism. Our drive for courtroom justice in the form of vindication is a powerful cultural and psychological force that contributes to the civil justice gap. Since NDR *also* delivers that vindication, and at costs which make sense, it would be reasonable to expect that our culture would *not* be one of the challenges to NDR's more widespread adoption. But culture is a multiheaded dragon. At least three aspects of our user culture present real obstacles to NDR:

- We're "lawsuit happy."
- We're inclined to defer to lawyers' opinions falling *outside* their expertise.
- We're apt to hear and obey the siren call of leverage.

Figure 11 depicts these three faces of the cultural challenge to NDR.

FIGURE 11 American Culture Challenge to NDR.

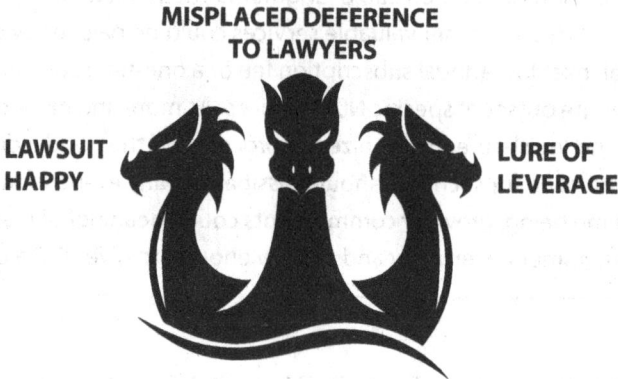

MISPLACED DEFERENCE
TO LAWYERS

LAWSUIT
HAPPY

LURE OF
LEVERAGE

I LOVE WHAT YOU GIVE ME

America *is* a lawsuit-happy culture: Don't tread on any of our "rights"—even rights we wouldn't intuitively expect, or which only exist because of someone's political judgment call or socioeconomic agenda—or else we'll sue. And we have lots of rights: human, constitutional, statutory, substantive, procedural, regulatory, equitable, judge-made, and imaginary. Just ask anyone from any other nation on earth which nation's people are most litigious.[14] We love winning, we love our rights, we love a good hero, and our adversarial justice system can deliver all three. What does it matter that this comes at costs in legal fees, distraction, stress, reputation, and relationships that dwarf the monetary value of the dispute? What does it matter that the fear and threat of lawsuit liability today intimidate us from exercising reasonable freedom and common sense in many daily activities and interactions?[15] And what about the unthinkable—the risk that we might actually be wrong and lose? What are all those costs worth if we lose?

Unfortunately, when circumstances call our lesser angels of anger or greed, we ignore or misjudge likely costs and risks. We've been brainwashed to think the only way to get justice in civilized society is to sue or threaten to sue, or to defend our actions and our character with everything we've got. Too often, we want a lawyer who will indulge—perhaps even profess to share—our triggered emotional outrage. Consequently, whenever we think someone is treading on our rights, and the innovation naysayers come to preach their "FUD" (fear, uncertainty, and doubt) about NDR, we're predisposed culturally to resist this useful innovation. 💡

BRIEF

FUD, the acronym for **fear, uncertainty, and doubt**, is a common expression and strategy that established companies use in competitive marketing to defeat or marginalize innovative competitors by suggesting, with little or no evidence, the possibility of harmful damage, embarrassment, or other negative consequences from trying or using the latter's products or services.

MISPLACED DEFERENCE

Many clients tend unquestioningly to accept their lawyers' advice about options and best paths forward without realizing that their lawyers' expertise is in fact *limited* by training and experience, while these decisions go well beyond the realm of legal expertise to en-compass a host of other important considerations and values. This uncritical reliance is yet another big challenge for real innovation in dispute resolution.

Some deference is perfectly understandable. In 21st century Amer-ica, the unprecedented acceleration in the pace of change in all aspects of our society—from information gathering and exchange to evolving knowledge in all fields—raises the difficulty of making good and timely decisions about *anything* without seeking specialized expertise. This is particularly evident in the field of law, where complexity and constant change in both substantive law and legal procedure justify, if not com-pel, getting professional advice and services in most situations—just as we do in fields like medicine, engineering, and technology. As in those other fields, however, the major decisions that we are called upon to make need to be educated and should reflect our own priorities, values, and beliefs as opposed to those of others. Consequently, there are al-ways questions we should ask and have answered in order to make the best-informed, best-for-us decisions we can. To that end, one informed commentator on the subject of better decision-making eloquently ex-pressed the reason for not relying entirely on superior expertise:

> Why would we *not* want to be governed [exclusively] on the basis of scientific expertise? Start with the fact that expertise is necessarily narrow. To be a nuclear physicist or to be a medical doctor takes years or decades of focus. It is rare for anyone to possess this high expertise in more than one field, impossible for anyone to have expertise in as many as ten. *But the problems we face are not presented in the silos that are necessary to gaining expertise.* There must be some art of coordinating the knowledge . . . that addresses our problems in their entirety.[16] *[emphasis added]*

BRIEF

In the field of medicine, for example, it's likely that most of us have faced situations that were improved or even better solved by therapies or other courses of treatment found outside the strict confines of Western medical practice.

While our reliance on expertise is understandable, it should not be unquestioning or complete. *We, as clients, should not defer to our lawyers in decisions that require balancing costs, time, peace of mind, relationships, reputations, stress, and other values outside legal expertise.* It's our responsibility in a fast-paced world of change to think about, ask about, learn about, and weigh paths outside the box of conventional expertise.

THE SIREN CALL OF LEVERAGE: AN ELEPHANT IN THE ROOM

Another powerful and common obstacle to parties agreeing on a fair and truly efficient resolution process is simply that *one of them may not want this.* Instead, one party may want to exploit perceived economic leverage or other unfair advantage to bully or cheat their way through successful confrontation.

Here are two examples. In disputes with subcontractors, some general contractors in the construction industry threaten (overtly or implicitly) to not invite those subcontractors to future projects, in order to extract otherwise unjustifiable concessions in additional work or time and materials costs. Similarly, some very wealthy companies and persons routinely and purposefully intimidate and overwhelm complaining vendors, partners, and customers with hard-line positions that effectively threaten the most expensive and burdensome legal onslaught possible, regardless of merit, in order to compel the other side's surrender of legitimate rights or claims.

Lest we think only the powerful do this sort of thing, another such practice is the willingness of hypocritical attorney crusaders for clients' "causes" to employ petty vandalism, knowing insults, and/or patent dishonesty in order to effectively terrorize, demean, or out-maneuver those with whom they disagree. 💡 Finally, there are the old-fashioned bribes or payoffs to witnesses, judges, and the like. It would be naïve to think this no longer happens today, although the obvious criminality and availability of other less risky means to gain unfair advantage make it less common in contemporary America than in centuries past.

BRIEF

I actually knew a psychopath attorney who, while being adept and civil in courtrooms, intentionally sought to terrorize an opposing business party by filthily abusing and clogging their office toilet while at a deposition and engaging in extraordinarily rude and discourteous behavior toward opposing counsel and witnesses—all apparently in order to encourage a bigger, faster settlement from decent people who were loath to have him back on their premises ever again.

Using unfair leverage has two problems. First, it morally dimin-ishes the abuser, as well as the overall decency and quality of human relations and culture. That's important to many of us, but frankly means little to the abuser and is often easily and stupidly rationalized as vengeance due anyway. Second, and more practically, these actions usually don't stay secret, so victims will eventually learn how to ex-pose, avoid, and/or defeat them (for example, by doing business with others instead, or, when that can't be helped, taking contractual pre-cautions)—not to mention that the reputation of the abuser as a desir-able trading partner will decline. Today, making use of unfair leverage is increasingly shortsighted and ultimately less profitable.

Unfortunately, this very human cultural reality and failing in our legal system lies less with lawyers who litigate than it does with the rest of us as clients and business advisors. Here's why. Lawyers have no ethical duty or training to advise their clients against the folly of using unfair but lawful economic leverage, sympathy, or other perceived advantage in legal disputes. Indeed, clients routinely *want* their lawyers to use every available advantage. Moreover, few litigators will risk the appearance of disloyalty and ire of their clients—not to mention likely loss of fees—to advise clients on the relative virtues of the Golden Rule or good business partnering. This simply is not within the purview or role of most litigators. The burden of seeing the light here—asking the right questions, intelligently foreseeing and minimizing the many and likely costs of disputes, and then making sound economic decisions—must fall on the nonlawyers in the room.

So while I believe that *all* lawyers ought—and should be compelled—to learn and timely share the fact and features of NDR in a timely manner with their clients, it's the clients and their business advisors who hold the key to shrinking the role of unfair leverage in the civil justice gap.

CHAPTER SUMMARY

- Neutral-driven resolution (NDR) faces challenges to broad adoption despite the many advantages it offers to consumers of legal services and the delivery of real civil justice.

- The need for *all* parties to agree to NDR is sometimes an insurmountable challenge—especially when distrust prevails after a dispute has arisen.

- The reduced opportunity for legal fees in limited stakes disputes is also a challenge—although the net impact should be nominal.

- NDR is unfamiliar to most lawyers and their clients, lies outside the box of lawyer training, and goes beyond state-mandated professional standards.

- The egos of American lawyers and clients, as well as cultural predispositions about dealing with legal conflicts, impose additional subconscious barriers to the growth and adoption of NDR.

"My fees are quite high, and yet you say you have little money. I think I'm seeing a conflict of interest here."

CHAPTER 10

FOR THE LAWYERS

This chapter is for my fellow lawyers—many of whom are completely open to ideas such as NDR. Like me, they often have felt trapped in a system and culture that *should* be able to deliver more real justice in common disputes, but somehow does not.

WHAT WILL THE NAYSAYERS ARGUE IN THE DEBATE TO COME, AND WHY WILL THEY BE WRONG?

When I started thinking about the civil justice gap and how NDR could seriously shrink it, I decided to write a handwritten list of all the reasons why NDR wouldn't work or wouldn't be adopted by those whom it could serve well. Two pages of one-line reasons later, I knew something about what I would be up against. Along the way, I've resolved many of the objections, especially those focused on developing a process that would live up to its promise. The discussion of challenges to NDR in the prior chapter and that to follow are essentially what's left of that original list, plus a few additional items that came to light along the way.

Unfortunately, the NDR debate, at least at first, will not be limited to the realities of the already-articulated challenges. Instead, naysayers, many of whom will not even recognize their biases, and almost all of whom will be lawyers, will latch onto traditional thinking to preserve the status quo. What follows are the arguments that I've heard or suspected, and why they're just plain wrong.

NDR doesn't preserve people's legal rights.

THE ARGUMENT NDR tramples upon invaluable, time-honored rights, such as the right of confrontation and cross-examination, the right to jury trial, the right to have someone argue for us, the right to compel discovery from opponents of facts that we believe may be helpful, and other procedural protections and substantive rights that may be overlooked in a non-adversarial neutral-driven investigation and analysis.

THE ANSWER When stakes are limited, accommodating *all* the procedural rights in traditional adversarial process is simply too wasteful and expensive, insofar as it tends to consume all that is at stake, except possibly the priceless vindication that we seek. Moreover, NDR, via the broad discretion of the agreed Neutral, in fact can preserve practical, affordable versions of all of these procedures, including the option, if desired, to decide critical disputed facts via a privately convened jury or focus group.

Mediation is a better tool than NDR.

THE ARGUMENT NDR is similar to mediation in speed and cost, but in NDR the parties and their counsel lose control over the process and outcome, which likely leads to worse results and lower overall satisfaction for the parties.

THE ANSWER What NDR and mediation have in common is that both use an agreed neutral to oversee a less formal, less expensive process than litigation or arbitration. NDR is in fact faster and cheaper than mediation, because truth-focused investigation by the Neutral replaces the discovery, procedural combat, and briefing by opposing legal teams that usually precede mediation. NDR's costs in time and money can also be fixed in advance so they're rational in light of the circumstances and limited stakes. Moreover, an NDR investigation leads to a principled decision, as opposed to mediation's usual outcomes of either a frustrating compromise or failure to settle, with the latter doing little more than adding to overall time and costs to resolution. In other words, if justice were a baby, NDR would have Solomon save her, while mediation would let him split her in half.💡

💡 BRIEF

Nevertheless, in some situations, mediation indeed can be the better tool, and splitting the baby may make sense, particularly if it's the only expedited process and outcome upon which the parties can agree.

NDR favors the haves.

THE ARGUMENT NDR may favor the wealthy and powerful by reducing the lawsuit threat leverage that attorneys for victims, consumers, employees, renters, the poor, seniors, minorities of all kinds, and other politically, socially, or economically disadvantaged parties can wield in order to level the playing field. In particular, NDR could compromise the threats and benefits of:

- Special recovery statutes that effectively punish those who have (or are deemed to have) taken unfair advantage of others and thereby offended important public policies

- The right to jury trial and its attendant natural empathy or sympathy for perceived underdogs

- Lower cost (to clients) of contingent fee legal representation

THE ANSWER NDR does not erase any advantages a party may have due to natural empathy, special statutes for protected classes, contingent fee legal representation, and the like. The NDR Neutrals can take those factors, laws, and circumstances into consideration as may appear applicable, fair, and reasonable. It's true, however, that removing all gamesmanship and leverage from the dispute resolution process benefits only objective truth and diminishes intimidation, prejudice, and unfair advantage for any side.

NDR favors the have-nots.

THE ARGUMENT NDR may unjustly favor the poor and perceived victims of society by enabling economically weaker parties to pursue their rights at far lower cost and risk of being intimidated or overwhelmed by superior resources. Since our laws and culture increasingly favor underdogs, opening the floodgates of claims to disadvantaged parties disables the field-leveling inherent advantages of size and resources.

THE ANSWER Again, removing all gamesmanship and leverage from the dispute resolution process benefits only objective truth and diminishes intimidation, prejudice, and unfair advantage for any side. The balance that this creates is as good for "haves" as it is for "have-nots," protecting each against the abuses of the other in the bringing and defending of claims. NDR admittedly does not strip away the right that a stronger party may have to refuse to deal in the future with anyone who has crossed it, but that is a reality which limits what *any* dispute resolution process can do. Fortunately, economically powerful parties today are increasingly finding that strong-arm practices come at a high price to reputation and make for poor business practice in the long run.

NDR promotes more disputes.

THE ARGUMENT NDR might *increase* the number of disputes seeking redress, because it will encourage rather than weed out weaker or smaller claims, and it may disincentivize early compromise settlements in favor of full investigation and decision.

THE ANSWER In fact, NDR dramatically reduces disputes by disincentivizing greed, convenient myopia, intimidation, and gamesmanship in parties and attorneys alike. Also, by reducing opportunities for triggering emotions and egos, it discourages dispute proliferation of all kinds *during* negotiations, investigation, and any ensuing analysis. It thereby promotes principled, early resolution of both legitimate and vexatious differences alike.

NDR isn't a universal solution.

THE ARGUMENT NDR's basic requirement of contractual agreement makes it ineffective in those disputes where either a necessary party refuses to agree to it or a critical third-party witness refuses to cooperate.

THE ANSWER It's true that NDR is not the solution for such disputes—just as it's not the solution for high stakes disputes in which the high costs of litigation are warranted. This is no reason not to propose and use NDR in those cases where it does make sense. The same argument has not diminished mediation, arbitration, or settlement conferences.

Proposing NDR may be perceived as weak.

THE ARGUMENT Threatening meritorious legal action that will be costly and burdensome for an opponent to defend delivers a strong message that may intimidate the uncertain, weak, or guilty. Proposing instead a less burdensome path for all may be viewed as a milquetoast stance that is unlikely to intimidate.

THE ANSWER Strong threats are like shouting: They'll work with some people, but will be dismissed by, or inflame, most others. By contrast, inviting a plainly fair process that will "let the chips fall where they may" is at once a message of strength and belief, as well as a statement of moral intention and rational goodwill (often when least expected). Moreover, it usefully tests the genuineness of the other side's belief and intentions, helps predict their likely behavior (via their reply), and may reopen a door to reassessment and rational dialogue.

Disappointed parties may reject any result they don't like.

THE ARGUMENT Judicial decisions and court-entered arbitration awards have the force and effect of law, which, if ignored, are readily enforceable in court. NDR decisions may not enjoy that privilege, and so may require costly efforts to enforce, or may even prove entirely unenforceable in some instances, based on some legislature's perception of public policy.

THE ANSWER All NDR decisions are based on a written contract, and therefore—like arbitration awards and signed written settlement agreements—should be fully enforceable in court. Some may even qualify *as* arbitration awards under applicable law, as suggested in Chapter 8. In all events, the legal costs of NDR judicial enforcement appear comparable to enforcing court judgments, and may include awards of attorneys' fees, expenses, interest, and even the complete costs paid by the prevailing party for the NDR process itself. Nevertheless, some attorneys will concoct arguments to void their clients' commitments and thereby create some risk of further proceedings, but that risk almost certainly will not be as great and expensive as the existing rights of disappointed litigants to appeal court judgments.

It's not clear that NDR will save enough to be worth the trouble.

THE ARGUMENT There's no proof yet that NDR will save as much time, money, and stress as is claimed, nor that—whatever those savings—they will be sufficient to deter us from the "safer" traditional paths to which we are accustomed.

THE ANSWER The logic of the pie chart explained in Chapter 7 is both compelling and irrefutable. The fair neutral-driven process that is NDR cuts through maneuver and gamesmanship by focusing on truth, uses one team to do what two or more did before, eliminates multiple rounds of formal pleadings, motions, briefs, hearings, and arguments across a broad spectrum of procedural and substantive issues, replaces depositions and discovery wars with interviews and neutral-driven cooperation, accounts for limited stakes, reduces stress and other hidden risks, and returns hundreds of productive hours to the parties and numerous noncombatants who have better things to do. This aggregation of increased efficiencies, like the simple physics on which it relies, has no choice but to be several times faster, cheaper, and less disruptive than adversarial process by every measure. **Figure 12** illustrates this point by adding to the testing laboratory's costs table from Chapter 1 a hypothetical NDR column for comparison. Of course, reliable data can only come from real-world experience—experience that parties must choose to have—in order to overcome the cultural brainwashing from which we now suffer.

FIGURE 12 My Clients' Financial Equation at the time of Mediation Compared with a Hypothetical Agreed NDR Process.

Item	Actual (as settled)	Projected (through trial)	NDR Estimated (through decision)
Stakes/Max. Recovery	$40,000	$47,000	$47,000
Legal Costs	-$35,000	-$75,000	-$13,000
Lost Work Time	-$8,000	-$18,000	-$3,000
Net Recovery or Loss	-$3,000*	-$51,000	$31,000
Duration	9 months	>1.5 years	5-7 weeks

* Clients' Net Loss later increased by $30,000 when the start-up dissolved after paying only $10,000 of the settlement

NDR outcomes may not be as just or reliable as court or arbitration.

THE ARGUMENT There's no reason to think, nor is there assurance, that NDR decisions will be as reliably just as going to court or arbitration, which are true competitions of ideas fought by skilled and highly motivated opposing teams.

THE ANSWER In limited stakes disputes, NDR outcomes are designed to have comparable reliability to litigation in court or arbitration, and overall will be better for all parties. Whether competing lawyers vie for supremacy, or a neutral-driven investigation is conducted by a skilled and mutually chosen Neutral, the underlying facts and applicable law are highly likely to emerge and control the outcome of almost all common disputes. This reality (and the great equalizing role of a neutral decision-maker) simply tends to overwhelm the impact of opposing lawyers in the vast majority of common disputes, even if one lawyer is a better advocate than the other. Moreover, in the remaining disputes—especially where stakes are limited— any such disparity in quality of counsel is extremely unlikely to make enough difference in the outcome to justify paying legal fees and other costs that consume most or all of the financial stakes. Finally, NDR has its own advantage in the search for reliable justice: the mutually selected, proactive subject-matter-expert and empowered investigating Neutral who has the specific mandate to find the truth, and not merely referee a contest.

BRIEF _____

Whatever process or forum is used, there will always be some small and roughly comparable risk that an outcome will not comport with factual truth or law due to insidious and difficult-to-control factors like mistake, hidden bias, or unfair advantage. Tools to mitigate that risk as much as possible are present to lesser or greater degrees in all dispute resolution methods compared in this book, with court at the top end of the spectrum, NDR just below, arbitration (because it doesn't allow appeal) further below, and mediation (because its success is a compromise driven by many factors) beneath the others.

NDR will benefit its purveyors.

THE ARGUMENT　Rob, your start-up company, Just Resolve, promotes and delivers NDR. Don't you stand to benefit the most from NDR's adoption? Aren't you and your credibility tainted by your financial stake in the success of this method?

THE ANSWER　NDR is not about *anyone* making more money. It's solely about improving the incidence of justice in America by greatly reducing *all* of the costs that prevent this from happening. *No one* will become rich suggesting, offering, or using NDR. It's not a patentable invention. It's not a valuable trade secret. It's not a copyrightable work or a trademarkable brand. It can be administered by anyone with integrity and basic legal training and experience. It can deliver probably 80% of its effective value in savings and deterrence just by being written into a contract—without the parties having to experience or pay for the actual process. And it can be used in almost any negotiation at no cost to gain moral high ground, take initiative, show strength, gather intelligence, and preserve dignity. In short, my only real taint is that of the true believer.

We've tried this before, and it didn't catch on.

THE ARGUMENT　NDR is not really new or much different from similar neutral-driven practices using different names, such as neutral fact finders, ombudsmen, and private judges, and those just haven't caught on in the United States. Consequently, trying or using NDR is likely to be a waste of time.

THE ANSWER Lumping NDR together with *any* prior efforts like
   those mentioned above is like comparing apples to oranges.
   First, the defining elements of NDR are very different. Second,
   its benefits consequently have greater value, number, and scope
   in the space where it can best serve. Third, the challenges of
   our time are greater—like the need for real solutions to the
   civil justice gap that can meet the pace of today's business,
   technology, social, and information advances. Finally, using
   NDR by specifying it in contracts *before* disputes even have
   arisen has been neither contemplated nor tried in addressing
   the civil justice gap until now. In all these respects, NDR
   truly has the potential of a "Blue Ocean Strategy" (from
   the powerful book of the same name by W. Chan Kim and
   Renée Mauborgne[1]) for meeting as-yet-untapped demand for
   improved civil justice through value innovation. As such, it
   deserves a real and prominent place in America's tool kit for
   resolving common disputes.

What's in it for us lawyers?

The paradigm shift for which I argue cannot succeed without real support from our lawyers. As our gatekeepers to all things legal, lawyers
have unique knowledge and legal training to help guide clients' choices, and they are potentially the best first phone call that a person needing legal advice can make.

The bottom line is that some lawyers will openly or subtly oppose
NDR until they fully understand it. Even then, some will still fear and
oppose it—doing whatever they can to prevent or minimize possible
negative impacts on their practices.

In fact, their horrible scenarios are imaginary. Here are seven key
reasons why lawyers *should welcome* this innovation with enthusiasm
and seek to optimize its use *wherever and whenever it makes sense*:

- **NDR is good for our clients**—for their money, their time and energy, their dignity, their reputations and relationships, their peace of mind. In other words, with NDR in our active tool kits, we will better serve our clients.

- **Proposing NDR helps us get better net results for our clients in negotiations** when we (or our client) believe that our side is in the right and should win. In fact, even if that belief turns out to be wrong and our client loses on the merits, we will have obtained that better net result because using NDR will have cost far less money, time, and face to learn from mistakes made.

- **Proposing NDR when appropriate earns client loyalty** by *proving* that we put their interests first, while informing us valuably about our adversary. If it's rejected, it allows us to proceed traditionally with a clear conscience that we did all we could to avoid undue time and expense.

- **NDR is good for our legal practices**. It helps litigators by enabling focus on larger and more lucrative matters and better handling (such as referral to NDR) of uneconomic matters, with the potential to increase clients' trust, net results, and overall satisfaction. It similarly helps transactional attorneys by reducing the incentives and opportunities for any party to pursue unnecessarily costly disputes and, when disputes cannot be avoided, their many costs and adverse consequences to the clients.

- **NDR is good for our profession's reputation in society**. In fact, it directly refutes and shrinks our sad reputation for undue greed and provocation.

- **NDR is good for growing cross-border business** with persons and companies who fear, loathe, or philosophically object to our unduly expensive and confusingly complex system of justice.

- **NDR is good for society**. It helps close the civil justice gap for poor and wealthy alike, and it helps optimize everyone's precious resources of time, energy, and money, yet it still preserves our right to seek vindication when we choose, all while reducing the proliferation of destructive anger, hate, and resentment.

NDR cannot trump culture.

THE ARGUMENT As discussed in the previous chapter, we love a good fight, especially a battle between good and evil, and we abhor the idea of someone taking unfair advantage of us. We romanticize courtroom "showdowns" where justice is won. We define winning and losing by the vindication of our rights. So why should we agree to something that denies us such visceral satisfactions?

THE ANSWER Once again, the explanation is a host of reasons that together reveal the lunacy of wasting our time, money, and energy on traditional adversarial process when it doesn't make economic sense:

- If we're entitled to vindication, neutral-driven process is about as likely as adversarial process to both deliver it and minimize the risk of someone taking unfair advantage.
- Neutral-driven process protects both sides against the very likely prospect and costly evil of overestimating the chances of success.
- The process accommodates each party's need to be fully and fairly heard, and the satisfaction, trust, and dignity that come of that.
- Win or lose, neutral-driven process dramatically reduces the excessive costs and other negative consequences of our mistakes,

our blind spots, our egos, our emotions, our injuries, and also *our lawyers'* blind spots, egos, and conflicts of interest. In short, it enables real justice.

- Less than 10% of lawyer-driven disputes survive to trial or judgment of any kind, leaving us *more than 90% of the time* with neither the experience nor the vindication we first sought.

- What actually happens in courtrooms is *much* slower, more ambiguous, and usually far less satisfying than we have imagined and seen in scripted entertainments of all kinds. The real world of civil justice is not *Boston Legal* or *The Good Wife*.

- Agreeing to a fair and efficient neutral-driven method for resolving a dispute is enlightened business practice that enhances the reputations of *both* sides, preserves mutual dignity, teaches grace, reduces the risks and consequences of emotionally triggered escalations, creates a greater potential for early negotiated resolution, and may even salvage a valued relationship. In sum, it redefines winning in all the ways that winning ought to be redefined, and at least occasionally makes room for two in a win-win situation.

- Simply *offering* to agree to a plainly fair and efficient neutral-driven method for resolving one's dispute takes the moral and strategic high ground. This delivers a strong message of conviction, reveals much of value about our opposite number, and may open the door to settlement or other swift reconciliation.

- Even in those few situations where a courtroom showdown is likely to deliver the visceral satisfactions that we crave, does achieving them in that way really outweigh all the above considerations *and* the absurd (relative to stakes) legal and hidden costs of chasing them?

I submit that there is only one answer to the above question. If you disagree, you need read no further. If you agree with me, then it's time to act.

CHAPTER SUMMARY

- NDR faces not only real challenges to adoption but also naysayer arguments that some lawyers will offer. This chapter identifies and answers these arguments.

- The naysayer arguments cover a wide range of speculation, from NDR's impact on legal rights and justice to its effectiveness compared with mediation and arbitration, and also to who will benefit most and how.

- In each instance, the speculation is unfounded, overblown, or inconsequential.

- NDR is indeed good for clients, justice, lawyers, and society in general.

"It's supposed to ward off frivolous lawsuits."

CHAPTER 11

WHAT YOU CAN DO, AND HOW TO DO IT

"Always do what you are afraid to do."
—Ralph Waldo Emerson

In the terrific 1976 movie *Network*, a riled up network news anchor-man played by Peter Finch exhorts his live TV audience over and over to go to their windows and shout, "I'm mad as hell, and I'm not going to take this anymore!"[1] Within minutes, people around the country are doing precisely as he asked.

Now I don't ask *that* here, though I sometimes think it would be appropriate. Instead, my sincere hope is that your journey through this book—even if you skipped ahead a bit—has made you at least open to, or curious enough about, the potential good that neutral-driven dispute resolution can do for all of us and for our civil justice system, our time, our money, and our peace of mind, that you may want to know where to get it and exactly how you can use it. Some of you may even want to know what you can do to advance NDR's use in general as a genuine means to increase the quantity, quality, and affordability of civil justice available to *all* in our society.

In this last chapter, we'll start with the *where*, move on to the *how* at a personal and practical level, and finish with some of the *whats* that can enable meaningful change for everyone.

WHERE CAN I GET IT?

There is more than one way to do NDR and more than one context for its use, so as you might guess, there is also more than one place to get it. Current models and providers for NDR include:

1. Dispute Resolution Boards (DRBs) used in large construction industry projects for mostly nonbinding recommendations. Neutral experts with experience and/or training in DRB investigations and facilitation may even be willing to perform NDR processes on a "one-off" basis in smaller construction disputes. These experts can be found through the Dispute Resolution Board Foundation (www.drb.org) and the construction practice of the American Arbitration Association. (https://www.adr.org/construction).

2. That form of "collaborative" divorce lawyering in which both spouses or domestic partners together retain the same attorney-mediator (and possibly other neutral experts) to investigate and recommend fair terms of their dissolution and division of assets. To find lawyers who work in this arena, consult the International Academy of Collaborative Professionals (www. collaborativepractice.com), or any comparable organization or reputable legal practice that offers this shared attorney-mediator option.

   Unfortunately, some collaborative law practices will *not* offer the shared attorney option, preferring instead that the parties separately retain their own attorneys who are tasked to collaborate in reaching an amicable resolution. This latter approach is easier on the attorneys—who are more comfortable with the obligations and undivided loyalty of traditional legal representation—but it multiplies legal costs and so is much harder on the divorcing spouses' wallets while greatly shrinking their net asset pool for division.

3. Certain membership, industry, and statutory processes designed to expedite the resolution of smaller disputes without need of adversarial process. The Better Business Bureau (www .bbb.org), for example, has long been a strong advocate of best business practices and offers an expedited and informal resolution service for smaller commercial disputes without need for dueling attorneys. Similarly, many state governments have departments or divisions which are dedicated to helping consumers expedite commercial, residential, and other kinds of disputes without requiring attorney involvement. In California, for example, there's the investigation arm of the California Department of Consumer Affairs (www.dca.ca.gov /enforcement). Also, if you are an investor in the United States

and you have a dispute with your securities broker, you can seek help from the Financial Industry Regulatory Authority's (FINRA) Office of the Ombudsman (www.finra.org /OMBportal) or, if the claim is under $50,000, FINRA's small claims mediation office (https://www.finra.org/arbitration -mediation/finras-mediation-program-small-arbitration-claims).

4. Independent neutral service providers who offer and administer binding or advisory NDR by one name or another. My own company, Just Resolve (www.justresolve.com), has pioneered and specializes in my preferred version of NDR. At least two other ADR services also expressly include forms of NDR in their offerings: Advantage Arbitration and Mediation Services (www.advantageadr.com/processes) offers NDR under the name Neutral Fact Finding. Anywhere Arbitration, Ltd. (www .anywherearbitration.com/how-it-works) offers what it calls fast online "arbitrations" conducted via email submissions that enable neutral-driven investigation. The landscape of providers offering NDR no doubt will evolve and grow as the method's usefulness and benefits become better known and disputing parties and client-centric attorneys ask for it.

5. Independent neutral professionals—including mediators, arbitrators, retired judges, neutral investigation services, and traditional ADR administrative services capable of readily assembling a basic set of appropriate NDR rules. Fortunately for them, we've done much of the legwork right here in this book.

In short, finding someone capable of administering a fair, reliable, and competent NDR process should not be difficult. The trick is getting opposing parties and their lawyers to see the light and agree to it. The following discussion describes how to make this happen.

WHAT NONLAWYERS CAN DO NOW

If you agree that it's time for change in resolving legal disputes—time for us and all other honest parties to get real and affordable justice, to recognize and stop the self-destructive side of our emotions and egos, to stop the greedy, the lunatics, and the manipulators from stealing our precious attention and money, and to keep our dignity and salvage relationships even when we're mistaken—here are seven simple, practical things you can do. In both business and personal situations, these can and will help you achieve all of the above (and make a real difference for others as well).

- **Propose NDR clauses in any written contracts you can, before any dispute arises.**⚲ This does several good things. You can start with my samples from Chapter 8 or customize with a lawyer's help. If your counterpart accepts your suggestion without controversy, you've just dramatically reduced the incentives and opportunity for intractable disputes to arise and the likely time and costs consumed if they do. You will have also substantially protected yourself against the mistakes, lunacy, intimidation, manipulations, and greed of others (and even, God forbid, yourself!), while making real justice attainable and highly probable if something goes wrong. It's almost like getting the easiest, cheapest litigation insurance you could ever have. Moreover, you will have taken the high road in communicating how you deal with people and what they can expect of you. If, on the other hand, your suggestion draws objection or difficult conversation, you will quickly learn valuable lessons about the persons with whom you are dealing.

BRIEF

Unless you run a business or other organization, you may not have many opportunities to include NDR in contracts. Often, we have little choice but to go along with whatever appears in a printed contract form. Most companies are loathe to entertain changes to their standard forms other than typically negotiated terms like price, quantity, and quality. Moreover, these companies have already paid lawyers to help them craft terms believed to be in their best interests, so we can expect push-back if we balk at those terms. Meanwhile, our time feels too valuable to spend on something that we probably won't need (few people sign contracts expecting a dispute), that we probably can't change anyway, and that's awkward or too poorly understood to bring up.

On the other hand, if you do run a business or other organization, you may have numerous occasions to consider and propose NDR in your contracts. Even employee contracts and handbooks can include NDR as an optional employee grievance procedure which, if both sides agree, may reroute potential lawsuits to a much better path and outcome for all concerned.

- **Whenever you face a legal battle over a limited stakes disagreement—either as the aggrieved party or the defending party—suggest NDR for resolving it, irrespective of whether lawyers are already involved.** If you have a lawyer, discuss the benefits and risks of this path compared with alternatives, *including estimates of total likely legal fees and hidden costs for each side.* If you don't have a lawyer and want help proposing NDR to the other side, contact an NDR service provider to do an initial dispute outreach. In any event, if NDR is offered and accepted, both sides likely will be much better off when all is said and done. Even if it's rejected, you may have reduced the other side's confidence while gaining insight into what is really motivating them, including whether they truly believe that they're right. At worst, you will have very effectively communicated your strong belief that you expect to win while taking the moral high ground that you have no desire to punish anyone beyond what's essential for you to obtain justice. In short, you have nothing to lose by suggesting NDR.

- **When facing *any* dispute situation, pause and challenge yourself (or your organization) to be creative, to try to see what the other side sees, and to recognize the uncontrollable potential for *anyone* involved—parties, witnesses, lawyers, assigned judges, arbitrators, and juries—to suffer blind spots like bias, resentment, desperation, greed, and irrational reactions due to triggered emotions and egos.** Doing so may well point you to the net value and benefits of a fair, fast, and inexpensive process like NDR. Even on the rare occasion when this self-analysis changes none of your plans or thinking in the moment, reflecting on the big picture will give you confidence in your decision-making going forward and help you avoid or minimize costly mistakes in the future.

- **Suspend disbelief.** NDR is NOT too good to be true; it really works. Like any worthwhile innovation, there's always a period of doubt that precedes acceptance. Consult early adopters of NDR regarding their experiences.

- **Beware the naysayers.** For example, just because your lawyer or another's lawyer isn't yet familiar with NDR doesn't mean you should defer to that ignorance. Also, be aware that some entrenched, powerful, and articulate interests may use fear, uncertainty, and doubt to argue against NDR. Judge their answers for yourself or with the help of someone who is knowledgeable, who undisputedly has your best interests at heart, *and* who has nothing to gain from whatever decision you make.

- **Talk with an NDR provider to learn more or to share your own past litigation experience.** As is the case in interviewing most lawyers before hiring them, NDR providers charge nothing for introductory calls to explore their neutral services, answer questions, or discuss potential situations where their services may be useful. At least one NDR provider, Just

Resolve, offers a free online calculator that estimates the potential total costs of litigating individual limited stakes disputes based on likely cost drivers vs. using NDR (https://www.justresolve.com/tcl-calculator/). **Appendix D** is the form of questions and answers from that online calculator. Just Resolve also uses visual tools such as user-friendly story boards to help explain how the process works. **Appendix E** is one of these.

- **Introduce NDR to your business, industry, service organization, or social network, either by asking "What about this idea?" or by inviting education and awareness via an NDR provider who can speak about it or submit an article.**

WHAT LAWYERS CAN DO NOW

Here are five ways attorneys can take action now to shrink the civil justice gap:

- In their capacities as legal advisors to their clients, lawyers can do the very same things that I have suggested to nonlawyers above, incorporating NDR as a valuable deterrent and anti-escalation tool in contracts and proposing it as an effective settlement remedy whenever it makes sense.

- Lawyers who are trained mediators and arbitrators, and eventually the major corporate ADR service provider brands (such as AAA, JAMS, etc.), should include NDR as a service offering and adopt and share simple, practical rules for executing the method.

- Lawyers and law firms need to educate themselves and their clients about NDR's merits and uses and actively encourage its consideration whenever it may serve the best overall interests of a client.

- Lawyers and courts should add NDR to mediation and arbitration as pre-trial ADR options in civil cases.

- Lawyers should lobby local, state, and national bar associations to add NDR to continuing legal education (CLE) programs that present or compare ADR methods, and to amend codes of professional responsibility to promote frank and full disclosure to clients of the advantages, risks, and likely costs of all available paths to conflict resolution.

SIDEBAR

Major ADR providers may be slow to include NDR because they fear cannibalizing their business model and alienating their primary customers—litigation attorneys referring highly profitable mediations and arbitrations. However, as client and lawyer demand for NDR grows, these providers should be well equipped to deliver it. Their existing infrastructures, reputations, and established panels of capable neutrals are easily adaptable to NDR, and they should be able to earn comparable fees driving robust independent investigations instead of playing reactive and comparatively passive roles as facilitators and adjudicators. Those who may ask why I, as a promoter and purveyor of NDR, would welcome such potentially devastating competition from the 800 lb. gorillas of the ADR industry will be missing the point of this book.

FROM SMALL STEPS TO GIANT LEAPS— WHAT <u>WE</u> AS A SOCIETY MUST DO

If, as described above, each of us has the power to make a real difference in closing the civil justice gap for ourselves and those with whom we work, imagine the speed and impact toward more universal justice if even a few of our institutions and most powerful constituencies were to follow suit. Here is a first take on what those steps would look like and who needs to take them:

- Law schools need to teach NDR, the justice gap that it addresses, and the concept of creative "outside-the-box" problem-solving in which lawyers may play invaluable roles without driving up costs and micromanaging every process using the tools of traditional advocacy. It's very simple to add NDR to now-common student classes in ADR (Alternative Dispute Resolution).

- Our *general* education should encompass the psychology of relationships and conflict, including what happens to our perceptions and judgment of others when we are "triggered" by anger, hate, resentment, and other negative emotions, along with the counter techniques for righting ourselves and "playing well with others" for win-win mutual benefit whenever possible. In other words, as citizens of an ever more populous and faster-moving world, we must learn how to better recognize and overcome our biases and darker impulses.

- Legislatures should enact laws encouraging, enabling, and enforcing NDR where parties freely have so agreed—much like the legal stature now accorded arbitration.

- Lawyers, governments, companies, and industry organizations should gather, share, and study experiential data (including comparative costs vs. outcomes by process) that will truly enable better and more informed decision-making by clients at the outset of disputes. This can be done without compromising attorney-client confidentiality and privacy. Data can be submitted and sorted anonymously, as is typically done with most epidemiological studies.

- Where appropriate, government agencies of all sizes and kinds should take advantage of the *free* goodwill and efficient dispute management that comes with including NDR in written vendor, purchaser, and service contracts for whatever the parties can agree would be limited stakes disputes as defined in this book. Similarly, governments should examine the kinds and sizes of common disputes that would be more efficiently and justly resolved via NDR (or an Ombudsperson) than through protracted taxpayer-funded litigation. (Unfortunately, it won't be many governments who initiate this examination and change, as most jealously guard their huge taxpayer-funded advantage in dealing with individual citizen and business complaints.)

- Insurers should recognize and offer NDR with incentives (such as lower premiums and faster claims handling) as an alternative to litigation for resolving modest claims.

- Employers should offer NDR from truly neutral, independent providers to all employees as an optional grievance process. Only then will employer protests about attorney-inspired extortion, "piled-on" liabilities, and the injustices of punitive class actions probably gain traction to re-level the playing field in the direction of greater fairness and efficiency going both ways.

BRIEF

Additionally, someone—perhaps an influential leadership or other organization, or perhaps a group of prominent businesses, insurers, or even ADR/NDR providers—may eventually create and promote a broad virtual "society" or other online community whose members pledge to use NDR to resolve limited stakes disputes whenever practicable.

LAST WORDS

Our system of adversarial justice has the best of intentions, but when stakes are limited, both organizations and individuals, regardless of wealth, must increasingly either forego valuable rights or allow themselves to be led like calves to the slaughter of too-costly litigation. Neither path leads to justice. The consequence is today's growing civil justice gap.

Many clients and lawyers believe there is no good and practical solution to this gap. They are misled. Neutral-driven resolution *is* such a solution. This book has sought to explain why and how that is so, and what we can do to bring NDR into our lives. But even convincing explanations and wise prescriptions are worthless if for whatever reasons, we don't act on them. So I ask all of us, both clients and lawyers, to act. Act despite fear. Act though acquiescing to the *status quo* seems easier. Act by redefining "winning" better and smarter than our reptilian survival instincts and lawsuit-happy culture tempt. Act so that tomorrow delivers more justice at reasonable cost.

CHAPTER SUMMARY

- NDR is currently available in several contexts from different sources.

- Nonlawyers can get NDR and promote its growth by writing it into contracts, suggesting it during dispute negotiations, asking their lawyers about it, asking an NDR provider to reach out to the other side when disputes arise, and inviting education, conversation, or presentation about it.

- Lawyers can get NDR for their clients and promote its growth by doing each of the above, and also by proactively considering and discussing it as an option with clients whenever it makes sense, by encouraging NDR's inclusion in ADR programs in court and industry, by serving as NDR neutrals, and by lobbying bar associations to improve rules of professional responsibility.

- As a society, we can substantially close the justice gap by rendering justice more accessible and affordable for all, *if* influential institutions like law schools, schools of general education, government agencies, employers, insurers, and legislatures evolve to teach or use NDR principles in key aspects of their respective curriculums or operations.

APPENDIX A
Glossary of Legal Terms

ADR: the acronym for alternative dispute resolution.

adversarial process: that method of resolving disputes principally employed by courts and popular ADR forums in the United States and Great Britain. Adversarial process is a competition—usually driven by opposing attorney teams on behalf of clients—to investigate, prepare, select, and present evidence and arguments to a neutral decision-maker such as a judge, jury, or arbitrator, with a view to obtaining the most favorable possible outcome for the client.

alternative dispute resolution: a process in which a neutral third party helps disputing parties resolve their differences outside of court. Common forms include arbitration, mediation, neutral evaluation, and settlement conference.

arbiter: a neutral person with authority to settle or decide a dispute.

arbitration: an ADR adversarial process like litigation, usually defined by statute and conducted privately, in which the parties agree to submit a dispute for a binding or nonbinding decision to one or more arbitrators.

arbitrator: a neutral person who presides over and decides an arbitration.

attorney-driven or lawyer-driven process: any adversarial process in which opposing attorneys lead and conduct their client's investigation, research, analysis, and presentation of a dispute, characterized by attorneys' advocacy and maneuvering for advantage for their respective clients.

bar: the institution of the legal profession, or the collection of attorneys authorized or licensed to practice in a court. It derives from the Latin root for "barrier" and first came into use during the Middle Ages as the physical (usually wood) bar separating the public from the working areas of a courtroom.

benefit of the bargain: the right to receive what the other party to a contract has promised to perform or deliver.

civil court: a court that handles noncriminal matters such as lawsuits between parties.

civil litigation/lawsuit: a noncriminal legal action.

class action: a lawsuit brought in the name of representative member(s) of a group of people to right a claimed wrong that all members of the group may have suffered similarly and in a way that common issues and proof may outweigh individual differences for purposes of the efficient administration of justice. Most states have statutory schemes enabling such lawsuits.

client-centric attorney: an attorney who advises and acts with intent to serve the client's overall best interests without regard to his or her own interests in earning fees, fame, etc.

collaborative law: a cooperative process for resolving legal issues between parties who agree—usually with specially trained attorneys—to seek a fair, principled, and cost-effective resolution rather than advantage over the other party. Collaborative law is most commonly found in the contexts of family law and divorce.

common law: a body of law based on written judicial case precedents, as opposed to law created by statutes. The United States, Great Britain, and most countries that were part of the British Empire are considered common law countries.

contingent fee: a lawyer's fee for legal services that depends on success, typically agreed in advance as a percentage of the value or amount of money actually recovered for the client.

criminal law: the law pertaining to crimes.

defendant: the responding or accused party in a civil lawsuit or criminal prosecution.

deposition: a formal question and answer session of a witness under penalty of perjury, usually in an attorney's office, taken as part of discovery in a civil or criminal legal action.

discovery: a formal pre-trial process of factual investigation in a civil or criminal legal action that commonly includes written interrogatories (questions), production of documents and objects, requests to admit, and/or depositions under oath.

enforce or enforcement: the legal term for the authority and act of a court to require a party to comply with a valid court order or judgment.

forum: a place, either physical or virtual, for exchanging ideas and views on an issue, including a court.

injunction/preliminary injunction: a kind of court order that prohibits or mandates specified conduct by a party in litigation.

Inns of Court: professional associations for barristers in England and Wales. Every barrister must be a member of one of four established Inns.

interrogatories: written questions submitted in discovery by one party in a lawsuit to another, requiring answers under oath.

legal costs: professional fees and related out-of-pocket expenses spent by parties on lawyers, neutral professionals, experts, courts and/or alternative forum providers.

liquidated damages: fixed or formulaic payments prescribed in a written contract for use in the event of specified kinds of breach of that contract.

litigant: a party or one of the "sides" in litigation.

litigation: the adversarial process, usually attorney-driven, of resolving a legal dispute through formal legal action such as a lawsuit.

litigation attorney/litigator: the kind of lawyer who advises on, manages, argues, settles, and, when necessary, tries cases for clients, as distinguished from, for example, an attorney who works on transactions or estate planning.

mediation: an ADR process in which a neutral third party facilitates settlement discussions.

mediator: the neutral third party who facilitates a mediation.

merits: who is right and should win a dispute given the pertinent facts and applicable substantive law.

NDR: an acronym for neutral-driven (or non-adversarial) dispute resolution.

neutral-driven (or non-adversarial) dispute resolution: an ADR process in which the disputing parties agree to a cooperative, truth-focused investigation and decision of their differences conducted by a neutral third party, instead of an adversarial process driven by opposing attorney teams.

neutral fact-finding: a dispute resolution tool by which a mutually agreed expert investigates and may decide key disputed fact issues chosen by the attorneys or a judge in the course of litigation.

non-adversarial process: a method of doing something characterized by cooperation and collaboration in seeking a principled outcome, as distinguished from a competition between opposing sides.

ombudsman: an official appointed by a government or other organization to investigate complaints against people in authority.

party: a person or organization who either has entered into a contract, or is named in a lawsuit or other legal dispute as a plaintiff/claimant or defendant/respondent.

perjury: the act and crime of lying under oath.

plaintiff: the complaining party in a civil lawsuit.

procedural law: sets of rules that govern how a court and the parties conduct a legal proceeding.

punitive damages: also known as "exemplary damages," an amount of money awarded in a civil lawsuit in order to punish the defendant, in excess of damages awarded to compensate the plaintiff for loss.

requests to admit: a tool of formal written discovery in a civil lawsuit that asks an opposing party to admit certain facts or legal conclusions.

sidebar: in law, a discussion in a courtroom among the judge and opposing attorneys conducted outside the hearing of the jury, witnesses, and public.

stakes: the value or amount in dispute, usually measured in dollars; more specifically, it is the total difference in dollars between opposing parties' sincere positions. For example, if Jake believes Bill owes him $30,000, while Bill denies this and instead believes that he is owed $5,000, the stakes are $35,000.

subpoena: a written order, usually issued by a court, for a witness to give testimony on a particular subject or allow inspection of a document or thing.

substantive law: the laws that define and govern the rights and obligations of people and organizations in given factual circumstances.

tentative ruling/decision: a preliminary ruling indicating and explaining a decision that a judge intends to make in a legal dispute, absent subsequent persuasion otherwise by one of the parties.

unjust enrichment: unfairly keeping a benefit received from another without paying for it in circumstances where the benefit was not intended as a gift.

APPENDIX B
Sample Agreement to Arbiter, Scope, Fees, Rules

APPENDIX B: PARTIES' SAMPLE AGREEMENT TO ARBITER, SCOPE, FEES, RULES
(parties' and persons' identities have been changed to protect their privacy)

JUSTRESOLVE
CURE FOR THE COMMON LAWSUIT

Thomas Tort, President
Drug Development, Inc.
555 East Coast Avenue, 5th Floor
Boston, MA 02210
Telephone 508-555-5555
ttort@ddi.com

Betty Bettencourt, Vice President
Biologic Testing, Inc.
444 Hitech Drive
Innovation, CA 95555
Tel 213-555-5555
bbettencourt@bti.com

FEBRUARY 2, 2020

Agreement to Arbiter and Fee *re:* Delay Misunderstanding; Study No. BT22-222MA

Ms. Bettencourt and Mr. Tort:

This confirms that you have agreed in the above-referenced study contract (attached as Exhibit 1) to promptly and inexpensively resolve misunderstandings arising between you by using Just Resolve's non-adversarial method and rules. A copy of Just Resolve's rules and method flow chart are attached (as Exhibit 2) and are a part of this agreement. In this instance, the parties have agreed to mediate[1] before any decision is issued. Also in this instance, the parties agree that the obligation of confidentiality provided in Rule 16 does not apply.

Brief Description: Biologic Testing claims that the study sponsor, Drug Development, owes $28,064 in contractual charges and expenses for postponing the start of the subject study. Drug Development asserts that the study was not postponed, a unilateral assessment of a postponement penalty is inconsistent with the subject study contract, the timing of the subject study start was solely attributable to Biologic Testing, and, in any event, denies owing the claimed additional charges and expenses.

Just Resolve submits for your consideration and acceptance the following Arbiter and fee schedule. The Arbiter has been vetted for integrity, reputation and experience in neutral dispute resolution, and against potential conflicts of interest.

Proposed Arbiter: Harold Hart. (His CV has been previously provided or is enclosed with this letter.)

---

[1] I.e., participate in an informal negotiation facilitated by the neutral arbiter

Just Resolve Letter Agreement with BTI and DDI, February 2, 2020, page 2

Schedule: The Arbiter and parties intend to cooperate to complete the Resolve within two weeks after this agreement is signed and both parties' initial payments have been made. The Arbiter and parties will consult on specific scheduling that will accommodate the reasonable needs of each.

Proposed Total Fee *Per Party*: $1,400. 50% is to be paid to Just Resolve, LLC, upon signing this agreement. The balance is due within 30 days after settlement closes or final decision issues. Just Resolve guarantees that the total fee will be sufficient to complete the resolve process for the described misunderstanding. Any change in the claims of the parties or scope of misunderstanding must be subject to further written agreement.

EACH OF THE UNDERSIGNED PARTIES AGREES TO THE ABOVE TERMS AND AUTHORIZES THE PROPOSED ARBITER TO INVESTIGATE, MEDIATE, AND IF NECESSARY RENDER A BINDING DECISION CONCERNING THE DESCRIBED MISUNDERSTANDING IN ACCORDANCE WITH JUST RESOLVE'S RULES AND METHOD AND THE ARBITER'S GOOD FAITH JUDGMENT AND DISCRETION.

Drug Development, Inc.

_____   _____
Thomas Tort, President   Date

Biologic Testing, Inc.

_____   _____
Betty Bettencourt, Vice President   Date

Just Resolve, LLC

_____   _____
Rachel Rawlings, Vice President   Date

Enclosures (study contract, rules, CV)

JUSTRESOLVE
CURE FOR THE COMMON LAWSUIT

111 North Market Street
San Jose, CA 95113
855-280-2588

EXHIBIT 2: TERMS OF SERVICE AND RULES FOR RESOLVES
(rev. February 2018)

1. **Agree Whether to Be Bound.** The parties agree to submit their dispute for definition, investigation and non-adversarial resolution to Just Resolve, LLC ("Just Resolve") in the manner described in these Terms of Service and Rules ("Rules") and on any additional reasonable terms as the parties agree in writing, or which Just Resolve may adopt. The outcome will be binding on the parties, with the final decision enforceable in court, unless they have previously agreed in writing to a non-binding advisory-only process which typically will conclude upon issuance of the tentative decision of the Neutral Arbiter(s) ("Arbiter"). If and to the extent allowed by law, the resolution process and final decision described in these Rules shall be accorded the respect of an arbitration and award, respectively, for purposes of enforcement in court, and, when employed by the parties pursuant to a pre-dispute or other written agreement to "arbitrate," the process will be conducted in compliance with applicable law governing arbitrations, with the Arbiter(s) functioning as arbitrator(s). Whether the outcome is binding or advisory, the process may be referred to as a "Resolve" or "Resolve arbitration," and the parties must in good faith engage in and complete it before commencing any legal action in court on subjects within the scope of their agreement. The parties further agree that Just Resolve has jurisdiction over the entirety of the dispute.

2. **Cooperate Fully.** Each party must cooperate promptly and fully with every lawful request or direction from Just Resolve and, once selected, the Arbiter(s). If a party fails to cooperate, the Resolve may proceed and the Arbiter(s) may complete the investigation and render a tentative or final decision or award on the assumption that any information lost, withheld, delayed or destroyed was unfavorable to the uncooperative party. If an Arbiter requests access to trade secret or other confidential information, the Arbiter and Just Resolve will cooperate with that Party reasonably to protect the confidentiality of the information.

3. **Select Arbiter(s) and Experts.** After conferring with the parties, Just Resolve will recommend one or more candidates for Arbiter(s) and any needed subject matter experts ("Experts"). All candidates must be persons who have never been employed by either party, are qualified by experience or education to decide or help decide the dispute, and do not have a direct or indirect interest in either party or the subject matter of the dispute. If the parties cannot agree on a selection, Just Resolve will submit a list of at least 3 qualified candidates for that role, from which each party may reject only one. The parties must then accept Just Resolve's choice of one of the remaining candidates submitted, unless good reason is given in advance to believe a candidate so chosen cannot be fair and objective. If, before completing his or her assignment, an Arbiter or expert previously accepted by the parties becomes disabled, resigns for any reason, or is dismissed for cause, the parties and Just Resolve will replace that resolution team member as soon as possible in the same manner provided for initial selection, and will reasonably adjust the schedule accordingly.

4. **Designate Your Resolve Manager.** At the beginning of the Resolve, each party designates in writing a Resolve Manager. If no one is so designated, the highest executive officer or manager of the party serves by default. The Resolve Manager has both responsibility and authority to communicate with Just Resolve and the Arbiter(s) on behalf of the party, including to obtain and disclose requested information, arrange witness cooperation, and make binding decisions for the party pertaining to the Resolve. The Resolve Manager must be reasonably available during normal business hours. Either party may replace its Resolve Manager by notifying Just Resolve in writing.

5. **Follow the Schedule.** The parties must follow the schedule and process set by Just Resolve and the Arbiter(s). Unless otherwise agreed, the process is that described in **Attachment 1** below. The parties will be consulted about the schedule before it is set. Thereafter, each party must make best efforts to meet all deadlines. The Arbiter(s) may find any continuing or repeated failure by a party to

JUSTRESOLVE
CURE FOR THE COMMON LAWSUIT

meet deadline(s) to be a material breach of the duty to cooperate and subject to the consequences of noncooperation described in Rule 2 and/or the "Other Disputes" process of Rule 23. Just Resolve, the Arbiter(s), or the parties by agreement, may extend deadlines as fairness or circumstances warrant.

6. **Share Materials and Testimony.** Unless specifically identified by the disclosing party as highly sensitive and confidential, and agreed to be such by the Arbiter, all materials and any recorded testimony submitted by any party to Just Resolve or to the Arbiter(s) shall be provided to the other party(ies).

7. **Mediate If Agreed.** If the parties have agreed to mediate their disagreement, the Arbiter(s) will choose the manner and timing and will conduct the mediation before preparing any tentative decision.

8. **Choose Whether to Appeal.** In a binding Resolve, within seven (7) days after the final decision, either party may give written notice of intent to appeal. The appealing party alone will pay Just Resolve for the appeal, in an additional amount set by Just Resolve not to exceed 100% of total fees paid by all parties for this Resolve. Two additional Arbiters – again selected according to Rule 3 – will review the case and may, by majority vote among all Arbiters, choose to investigate further and/or change the final decision. A final decision so changed replaces the original final decision for all purposes. If the original final decision required the appealing party to make a payment, then the full amount of that payment must be placed in escrow with Just Resolve at the start of the appeal, and will be released according to the final binding decision following appeal. Just Resolve will give reasonable notice of when fees for appeal are due. Just Resolve, in its sole discretion, may declare an appeal abandoned if any such fee or payment is not timely posted.

9. **Pay on Time for Service.** Unless otherwise provided in these Rules or agreed in writing with Just Resolve, the parties pay Just Resolve in equal shares for its resolution services, including quoted Arbiter and expert fees, and out-of-pocket expenses (e.g. on-line research, any video-taped interviews, copying, mileage, etc.). Except where impractical or otherwise agreed, Just Resolve will quote a fixed, "not-to-exceed," or estimated fees and expenses total at the outset of services, and the parties will each pay 50% of their respective total shares in advance as retention against final invoice. The remaining 50% will be due before the Tentative Decision is released by the Arbiter(s). If the parties agree to add a mediation step or other work *after* Just Resolve has quoted or set its fees, then they may be required to pay additional fees for the additional services. In any matter exceeding two weeks in duration, Just Resolve may issue progress invoices due within two weeks. Fees incurred on an estimated or hourly basis are subject to later revision and reconciliation at the conclusion of the Resolve. For smaller disputes of reasonably predictable effort, the parties may agree on a firm fixed or "not-to-exceed" fee with the understanding that the Arbiter may limit investigative and analytical resources to a level commensurate with the stakes. Unless otherwise agreed by Just Resolve and the Arbiter, where they and the parties have agreed to a fixed fee and the case is resolved prior to a final decision, the parties shall pay the full fee.

10. **Changes in a Resolve.** If, during the course of the resolve, Just Resolve or the Arbiter(s) determines the contracted price does not sufficiently cover the Arbiter's costs due to mistaken estimation of the amount of time needed, an unanticipated need to hire an expert or conduct unforeseen legal research, a later-added mediation step, or any other change costing less than 20% of the originally quoted price per party, Just Resolve may set, and each party will promptly pay, its share of the increased cost. If the change requires an increase in cost greater than 20% of the original quoted price per party, Just Resolve will submit a revised price quote requesting each party's written approval. If either party fails to approve, Just Resolve and the Arbiter may choose to proceed with the Resolve for the original quoted price without benefit of the additional hours, expertise or other expense.

2

11. Contacts with Arbiter(s). Direct contact by a party with Just Resolve, the Arbiter(s), or any other member of Just Resolve's resolution team for the purpose of meeting obligations under this Agreement or to communicate points of view about the dispute are both expected and proper, and each party is free to rely on whomever it wants to speak for it. However, the resolution team is directed to recognize and compensate in its efforts if it appears that one party may gain unfair advantage by relying on a party-aligned attorney, expert or other dispute resolution professional. Also, before the final decision, no party or representative will engage in any inappropriate contact with any member of the resolution team. Inappropriate contact includes private advice or communication about possible future business or social relations – and any other contact – that might seek unfair advantage or create the appearance of seeking unfair advantage in connection with the resolution of the dispute.

12. Representation. A party to a Resolve need not be, but has the right to be, represented by an attorney or other representative at any proceeding or hearing. An attorney also may serve as a party's advisor and/or Resolve Manager.

13. Legal Research. The parties agree that Just Resolve may have a paralegal or other legal professional not having a conflict of interest conduct independent legal research for and at the request of the Arbiter.

14. Arbiter(s) Role and Practical Judgments. Just Resolve, including the selected Arbiter(s) and any Expert, do not represent any party, but rather will have the role and objective to neutrally and in good faith seek factual truth and to fairly apply pertinent general principles of substantive law and equity in order to resolve the disagreement within a reasonable time and cost given limited financial stakes. This may sometimes require practical and common sense judgments, including about what facts to investigate and what conclusions to reach based on imperfect information. For example, in assessing the quality, weight and credibility of information obtained during the investigation, the Arbiter(s) may be guided, but is not bound, by formal rules of evidence.

15. No Professional or Consequential Liability. In light of Just Resolve's role and limitations described above, and to the extent permitted by law, the parties each waive and forever release, in advance, any and all potential legal claims and demands against Just Resolve, its Arbiter(s), its Experts and any other members of the resolution team (jointly "Just Resolve") for any potential misconduct arising in connection with these Rules or this Resolve, other than failure to act honestly and in good faith. The waived and released claims include claims for professional malpractice or negligence, breach of fiduciary duty, conflict of interest, breach of contract, libel or slander in the course of communicating theories, demands or assertions of one party regarding the other during the Resolve, and their like. Just Resolve and the parties also waive and forever release, in advance, any potential claims against each other for lost profits and consequential damages arising out of the Resolve process, except as specifically provided for in these Rules. In order to make these waivers and releases as effective as possible, the parties each waive the benefit of California Civil Code Section 1542 (and any comparable law in other jurisdictions) which provides that:

> A general release does not extend to claims which the creditor does not know or suspect to exist in his or her favor at the time of executing the release, which if known by him or her must have materially affected his or her settlement with the debtor.

16. Confidentiality in a Resolve. The parties agree that the Resolve process is confidential. All statements made during the course of the Resolve are made without prejudice to any party's legal position and are inadmissible for any purpose in any legal proceeding. Unless otherwise agreed in writing, the parties and Just Resolve:
a. Will not disclose offers, promises, conduct and statements to third parties, and

JUSTRESOLVE
CURE FOR THE COMMON LAWSUIT

b. Agree that offers, promises, conduct and statements are privileged and inadmissible for any purposes, including impeachment, under Rule 408 of the Federal Rules of Evidence and any applicable federal or state statute, rule or common law provisions.

17. **Parties May Jointly Terminate Services.** Subject to the provisions of paragraph 9 regarding payment for services, if at any time the disputing parties agree in writing, they may by notice terminate Just Resolve's services and owe only those fees for work and out-of-pocket expenses incurred or committed to date. If the parties are owed reimbursement of any fees already paid, Just Resolve will reimburse within 30 days.

18. **Just Resolve May Terminate.** If at any time Just Resolve decides in good faith that an unexpected obstacle (for example, the unanticipated involvement or lack of cooperation of a third party, or unexpected burdens to address employee or proprietary rights) impairs its ability to resolve the dispute as agreed, Just Resolve may terminate the Resolve without liability or penalty other than that it will reimburse the parties for any fees paid it to date, except for reimbursement to a party who previously knew and failed to disclose the material facts creating the obstacle.

19. **Breach By Party.** If a party breaks these Rules, including failure to pay Just Resolve's fees when due, then Just Resolve may, in its sole discretion, suspend any remaining work pending cure and/or it may exercise its other available rights under these Rules or at law.

20. **Satisfaction and Enforcement of Final Decision.** In a binding Resolve, after receiving the final decision and explanation, an indebted party has 30 days to fully comply (including payment of any other award made by the Arbiter), or else the decision will be enforceable in any court of competent jurisdiction. If the court substantially enforces the decision, the prevailing party is entitled to a further judicial award against the indebted party in the amounts of the prevailing party's actual attorneys' fees and costs of enforcement, and its share of fees and expenses paid to Just Resolve in connection with this Resolve.

21. **Resolve and Final Decision in the Absence of a Party.** Unless otherwise provided by law or contract, if a party fails or refuses to appear or participate cooperatively in the Resolve, or in any portion of the Resolve, (e.g., by ignoring a demand to resolve, failing to participate in good faith in Arbiter(s) selection, failing to pay its share of Resolve fees, or failing to cooperate with Arbiter requests) after having been given notice and opportunity, the Resolve may proceed and the Arbiter(s) may render a final decision on the basis of such evidence and information presented by the participating party as the Arbiter(s) may require for the rendering of a decision and which, if true, would support such decision. A binding final decision rendered under such circumstances is valid and enforceable as if all parties had participated fully.

22. **Payment of Fees By One Party Per Agreement or in the Absence of Other Party.** If one party pays the other's share of fees and costs for Just Resolve's services per agreement, statute or the other's failure to appear or cooperate, and a final decision is rendered in favor of the paying party, then that final decision or award may, upon request and if not prevented by law or agreement, include reimbursement of those fees and costs by the non-paying party. In addition, the Arbiter(s) may award against any party any costs or fees that are a proper part of any award with respect to the Resolve.

23. **Other Disputes Among Parties or with Just Resolve.** If a dispute arises between the parties about the terms or performance of this Resolve or the underlying agreement to use Just Resolve (excluding judicial enforcement under Rule 20), the parties agree to submit the dispute to the Arbiter(s) for a binding decision that may include an award of fees and costs of such process. The Arbiter(s) will choose the process, schedule, amount and allocation of any additional fee required. Any other dispute arising out of the performance of this resolve or the underlying agreement to use Just Resolve

4

(excluding judicial enforcement under Rule 20), including a dispute between Just Resolve and one or more of the parties, will first be presented for informal mediation to the Arbiter(s). The Arbiter(s) will choose the process, schedule, amount and allocation to each party and/or Just Resolve of any additional fees required. If the dispute is not settled, any legal action on it will be brought in San Jose, California, and the prevailing party will be entitled to recover its attorneys' fees and costs.

24. **Legal Actions.** Except as may be reasonably necessary to establish the facts and scope of Just Resolve's role and services to the disputing parties and/or the content and enforceability of any binding final decision issued, in any later legal action between or among those parties, (1) Just Resolve will take the position that communications and information that the parties shared with Just Resolve and the Arbiter(s) are not discoverable or admissible, but rather were in the nature of confidential and privileged settlement communications, (2) each party agrees to make no attempt to compel the Arbiter(s) or any Just Resolve employee's or contractor's testimony or production of documents originally provided by the other party, and (3) the parties agree that neither the Arbiter(s) nor Just Resolve is a necessary party in any arbitral or judicial proceeding relating to the Resolve or to the subject matter of the Resolve. The parties also agree to defend the Arbiter(s) from any subpoenas from outside parties arising out of this Resolve.

25. **Notices.** All notices will be in writing and comply with any agreement between or among the parties and/or Just Resolve, or applicable law. Absent agreement or law to the contrary, notices received before 5:00 p.m. during normal business hours are effective that day. Later notices are effective the next business day.

26. **Service.** When formal service of process of a demand, notice or other document is required by law or agreement, service must comply with that law or agreement. Except as so required, service under these rules is accomplished by providing one copy of the document to each other party and one copy to Just Resolve on behalf of the agreed or future Arbiter(s). Service may be made by hand-delivery, overnight delivery service, clearly identified email or facsimile, or U.S. mail. Service by any of these means is considered effective when the document is transmitted or deposited, except that when the method of service is by U.S. Mail only, three (3) business days shall be added to any prescribed period for response or compliance.

27. **Governing Law.** California law governs these Rules and any agreement(s) incorporating these Rules, except to the extent otherwise agreed in writing or specified by the Arbiter(s) in applying the choice of law that in fairness ought to govern the parties' dispute.

28. **Complete Agreement, Written Amendments.** These Rules, any referenced Attachment to them, and any Agreement explicitly incorporating them, are the entire agreement of the parties, supersede all other inconsistent written or oral statements, understandings, and other communications, and may be changed only in a writing signed by the party against whom the change is being asserted.

29. **Unenforceable Terms.** If any part of these Rules, any referenced Attachment to them or any Agreement explicitly incorporating them is illegal or unenforceable for any reason, it will be severed and the remainder given effect as near as possible to the parties' original mutual intent as expressed prior to severance.

30. **Meaning of Terms.** For purposes of resolving any ambiguities in the meaning of these Rules, any referenced Attachment to them, and any Agreement incorporating them, all will be construed as having been prepared by all of the parties.

JUSTRESOLVE

ATTACHMENT 1: ACTIVE RESOLVE PROCESS FLOW

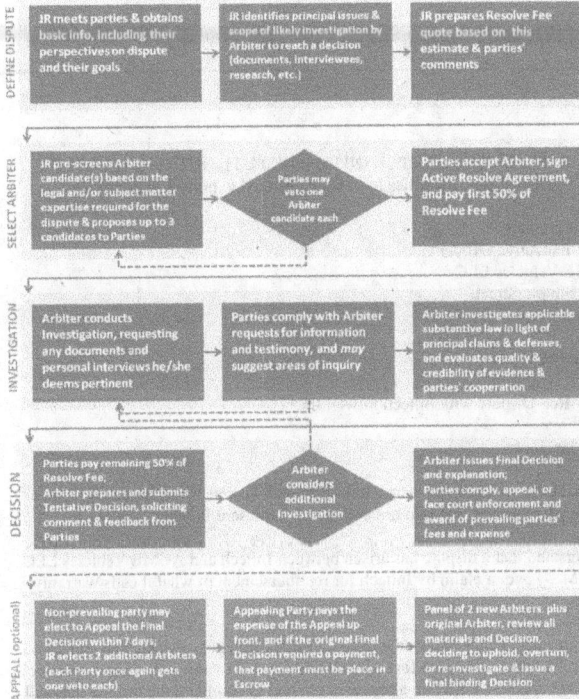

DEFINE DISPUTE	JR meets parties & obtains basic info, including their perspectives on dispute and their goals	JR identifies principal issues & scope of likely investigation by Arbiter to reach a decision (documents, interviewees, research, etc.)	JR prepares Resolve Fee quote based on this estimate & parties' comments
SELECT ARBITER	JR pre-screens Arbiter candidate(s) based on the legal and/or subject matter expertise required for the dispute & proposes up to 3 candidates to Parties	Parties may veto one Arbiter candidate each	Parties accept Arbiter, sign Active Resolve Agreement, and pay first 50% of Resolve Fee
INVESTIGATION	Arbiter conducts Investigation, requesting any documents and personal interviews he/she deems pertinent	Parties comply with Arbiter requests for information and testimony, and may suggest areas of inquiry	Arbiter investigates applicable substantive law in light of principal claims & defenses, and evaluates quality & credibility of evidence & parties' cooperation
DECISION	Parties pay remaining 50% of Resolve Fee; Arbiter prepares and submits Tentative Decision, soliciting comment & feedback from Parties	Arbiter considers additional Investigation	Arbiter issues Final Decision and explanation; Parties comply, appeal, or face court enforcement and award of prevailing parties' fees and expense
APPEAL (optional)	Non-prevailing party may elect to Appeal the Final Decision within 7 days; JR selects 2 additional Arbiters (each Party once again gets one veto each)	Appealing Party pays the expense of the Appeal up-front, and if the original Final Decision required a payment, that payment must be place in Escrow	Panel of 2 new Arbiters, plus original Arbiter, review all materials and Decision, deciding to uphold, overturn, or re-investigate & issue a final binding Decision

6

APPENDIX C
Sample Initial Dispute Outreach Letter

APPENDIX C: SAMPLE INITIAL DISPUTE OUTREACH LETTER
(the parties' identities have been changed to protect their privacy)

Mr. John Jones
Chief Executive Officer
ACME Vehicles LLC
5555 Simple Street
Santa Salvo, CA 95555

February 2, 2020

Re: Dispute with Initech Power, Inc.

Dear Mr. Jones:

I write at the invitation of Sam Smith of Initech Power, Inc. ("Initech"). I am an attorney by training, but I do not at this time represent Initech.

I understand that a dispute has arisen between Initech and ACME Vehicles LLC ("ACME") over a claim by Initech for reimbursement of what it calls warranty repairs.

If the two companies are unable to settle their differences quickly and amicably, and preferably *before* each formally retains counsel to advocate their respective positions in court, I offer an alternative method of resolving the dispute that will save each side many thousands of dollars in legal expense, not to mention the additional hidden costs and stress of litigation such as disrupted productive time, while assuring a process and decision as principled, fair and reliable as if the matter were decided by a sitting Superior Court Judge who routinely hears California commercial cases.

INTRODUCTION

Just Resolve LLC is a new service that provides swift, reliable, legal dispute resolution through agreed neutral investigation and decision in place of dueling attorneys in courts, arbitrations, or traditional mediations, at a guaranteed fraction of the cost to each side. How it can make this promise is described in detail in the description of Just Resolve's service and method enclosed with this letter, as well as on the "Services" and "FAQ" pages of the Just Resolve website at www.justresolve.com.

At Mr. Smith's request, I have read the most recent correspondence between your companies stating your respective (initial) legal positions, as well as what appears to be the operative independent sales agent agreement. This dispute makes sense for Just Resolve's method principally because (1) both sides appear to believe in the rightness of their perspective,[1] (2) the stakes are both meaningful and yet small enough that the likely expense to *each* side in traditional adversarial legal process would exceed the amount in controversy, (3) the parties are or should be more interested in truth and getting back to business than in sating frayed egos with costly victory or defeat, and (4) the facts and legal issues are subject to readily available expertise and a manageable and predictable scope of investigation and analysis. Of course, if either party must win at all costs even if those costs approach or dwarf the stakes, or if one truly enjoys the gamesmanship and quest for leverage inherent in the adversarial process, then Just Resolve is not for them and they should call in their separate advocates who will be happy to indulge those values.

If, on the other hand, you are attracted to the benefits of the Just Resolve alternative, please consider the following simple proposal.

PROPOSAL

The parties sign a contract, much like an agreement to arbitrate, in which they agree to a binding investigation and decision to be conducted by an experienced and *mutually acceptable* neutral "judge" (probably a retired California judge or senior partner/arbitrator with a prominent law firm) for an agreed or not-to-exceed total fee. In this case, based on apparent stakes of approximately $40,000 excluding possible statutory attorney's fees, the fee for *each* party could be set at or not-to-exceed $3,000. The judge follows Just Resolve's simple rules (which can be appended to the contract) to investigate and consider applicable facts and law, with the *intent* to reach the same decision on the merits that a court would.[2] The parties pay the fee in advance and cooperate with *every* request for interview and other information from the judge, offer whatever additional information they choose, read and respond to the judge's tentative decision, and then comply with the judge's final decision. If the losing party fails to comply, the prevailing party may enforce the decision in court, including the right to recover the fee paid to Just

---

[1] From my brief initial review of the dispute, it appears that the parties reasonably disagree on the law and likely will disagree on at least some potentially important facts. Your (or your attorney's?) letter of January 10 challenges Initech's good faith in asserting a claim, but if you have had experience in litigation, then you know that there are two sides to *every* story and that good lawyer advocates can articulate a reasoned and plausible -- if not compelling -- claim or defense for virtually any scenario.

[2] It is possible that the judge would need help from an expert or other professional, but in that event the person, qualifications, role, and not-to-exceed compensation also would be disclosed and agreed in advance.

Resolve and legal fees incurred in enforcing the contract. If the parties were to agree in advance, they may elect among additional, incrementally priced services like a pre-decision mediation or a losing party's right to an appeal or review of the decision by two additional judges.

In this instance, and because Just Resolve is a new company offering a new service, it will waive its separate case administrative fee in return for each party's participation in a post-decision survey and interview. Consequently, the parties will be charged only the standard rate of the professional neutral judge involved.

If ACME is either amenable to this alternative or interested in exploring it further, I invite you to call me directly at 408-555-5555 so that I may answer any questions that you have.

DISCLOSURE

My biography appears on the website. I met Mr. Smith about 15 years ago when I represented his former company, Big Co., in litigation. I have had no contact with him since then. I was unfamiliar with this matter until he contacted me about it last week. When I suggested Just Resolve, he agreed to it if you would as well.

CONCLUSION

The solution that I propose above will cost less to each of you (in every way) than the base cost of hiring an advocate to consult and strategize, review documents, research the law, communicate, and negotiate, regardless whether or not a legal action is ever prosecuted. I urge you to give it real consideration.

Very truly yours,

Robert A. Christopher
Chief Executive Officer
Just Resolve LLC
111 N. Market Street, Suite 300
San Jose, CA 95113

enclosure
cc Sam Smith (with enclosure)

APPENDIX D
Total Costs of Litigation Calculator Questions

Information about your dispute

1. In what **forum** will the dispute ultimately be resolved?

   ☐ Jury Trial   ☐ Judge Trial   ☐ Binding Arbitration

2. How many **different** people or organizations will be named as either a claimant or defendant?

   ☐ 2   ☐ 3   ☐ 4+

3. How many different **claims** seem likely?

   ☐ 1   ☐ 2   ☐ 3+

4. Are the main **issues** in dispute common or typical of disputes in your trade, industry or circumstances?

   ☐ Yes   ☐ No

5. Do you expect the parties to engage in mediation, nonbinding arbitration, or some other facilitated exercise to settle the dispute early?

   ☐ Yes   ☐ No

continued

Evidence questions

6. **What number of important witnesses likely will testify?**

   ☐ 2   ☐ 3-4   ☐ 5-6   ☐ 7+

7. How many important documents and other records likely will be used as evidence at trial?

   ☐ <10   ☐ 11-25   ☐ 26-99   ☐ 100+

8. **For one or more parties, how intense do you believe the dispute is or will become?**

   ☐ Low   ☐ Medium   ☐ High

9. How many technology, industry, and/or financial areas of **expert** opinion testimony likely will be needed?

   ☐ 0   ☐ 1   ☐ 2   ☐ 3   ☐ 4+

Financial questions

10. How much money is at stake in the dispute? $

11. What is your attorney's hourly rate $

Hidden litigation costs

12. What value, if any, do you place on the lost productivity that you and other personnel in your organization will suffer while distracted from regular work by litigation information gathering, meetings, other communications, preparation, depositions, trial, etc.? (Estimate days or hours diverted for each person by their compensation rate and add them up.)

$ _____

13. What value, if any, do you place on the additional stress and anxiety that you and others in your organization will incur while the dispute is pending?

$ _____

14. What value, if any, do you place on the risk that your organization loses a valuable relationship, or suffers some loss of reputation, because emotions escalate or perspectives diverge further during the dispute process?

$ _____

APPENDIX E
How Neutral-Driven Resolution Works

Two Parties have a legal dispute! Both are eager to **resolve it without the high costs** of dueling attorneys. Now what?

Normally if both sides cannot come to an agreement, attorneys are consulted. That can lead to early settlement, but if it doesn't, things can go sideways and become **expensive and frustrating**!

If both sides agree to use **Just Resolve**, we will recommend neutral Arbiter candidates with **expertise in the area of your dispute**. The parties agree on the Arbiter to use and have the option to retain their own attorneys to consult during the process.

The neutral Arbiter investigates and renders a tentative decision. Both parties can review and ask questions. The Arbiter then renders a final decision which is **fair and principled**, all at a fraction of the cost of traditional legal process.

ACKNOWLEDGMENTS

There are many people who played important roles—knowingly or unknowingly—in the creation of this book.

I owe thanks most of all to my wife Ginny. For over 40 years you have been there for me at every turn and in every way—including throughout this long book-writing project—giving sound advice, forever adapting to challenge and change, delivering support, peace, patience, and joy upon every homecoming, cheering me through my highs, and comforting me in my lows. That you've been able through it all somehow to maintain your own identity and relevance, do so much for others, and take the lead in raising our terrific sons, never ceases to amaze me.

I would be remiss if I failed to acknowledge also the foundation of support and joy that the rest of my family provides. While I've already written of the contributions of my Dad and Mom, I call out here the support of my brother and business partner, Bill, who has taken on the mantle of extending and growing our Dad's family farming business legacy and success to a new generation and who, along with my Dad, trusted my instincts in the legal arena and enabled my early exploration of NDR. My sons Jason and Tad, daughters-in-law Sylvia and Brittany, grandchildren Des, Willow, Cece, and Ruth, are constant and forgiving reminders that real love has no bounds and enables all.

I sincerely thank my fellow Vistage members over the past two decades who acted as an informal and caring advisory board to deliver inspiration, encouragement, input, and support in both my quest to find a solution to the civil justice gap and the form that the answer has taken. Special nods go to Dom Black, whose creative intelligence and enthusiasm for the cause has inspired me time and again, and to our chair Lance Descourouez, whose persistent encouragement and network of A-Team resources have empowered my efforts.

I thank my legal colleagues—both partners and opponents alike—and my many clients for the experientially rich career that I have enjoyed, for the encouragement of many of them in my current mission, and for their many valuable and relevant stories lived, lessons taught, and data contributed.

I thank my Just Resolve team—past, present, and future—for their belief in my mission to evangelize NDR and their many different contributions to it. Warranting special thanks are three people: First is Sonya Sigler, successful former in-house counsel and current business coach and author in her own right, whose business development efforts, introductions to key resources (including my primary content editor), general advice, arbiter recruitment, and commitment have helped give life to NDR. Second is Michelle McCulloch of Fusion Growth Partners, whose creative energies and talent spawned and crafted ever-better ways of telling the NDR story, including the story board that is Appendix E. Last is Most Valuable Player Jennifer Vessels, whose personal efforts and team at Next Step Growth have delivered structure, depth, butt-kicking and other discipline, improved strategy and business model, and high-quality content and illustrations in support of my NDR efforts generally and this book in particular.

Finally, I express my sincere and eternal gratitude to my book team. I hardly know how to begin to thank my principal content editor Ellen Bradley. A fine writer with legal training who "got it" from the outset, her contributions delivered extraordinary value throughout the writing process. She not only edited early and later drafts of the manuscript for content and style, but even went so far as to lighten my load by researching and writing the first draft of the chapter on legal history, much of which has survived into the final product. Similarly, it's difficult to adequately honor the contributions of Linda Popky and her team at Leverage2Market Associates (including book designer Jeanne Schreiber and cover designer Adam Renvoize), whom Jennifer Vessels recommended to oversee the publication process. Linda's resources, book publishing experience, project management skills, and patience with this over extended first-time author were exceeded only by her editorial savvy, diligence, and quick immersion in a difficult and alien subject matter.

NOTES

CHAPTER TWO

1   Like a "B.A.," the "A.B." is Stanford's version of a Bachelor of Arts.

CHAPTER THREE

1   Lloyd Duhaime, "China: A Legal History," *Duhaime Legal Information Corporation*, August 2008, http://www.duhaime.org/LawMuseum /LawArticle-363/China--A-Legal-History.aspx.

2   Claude Johns, "Babylonian Law: The Code of Hammurabi," *Encyclopedia Britannica*, 5th ed. (1910-1911), https://avalon.law.yale.edu/ancient /hammpre.asp.

3   Ibid.

4   Ibid.

5   Ibid.

6   William C. Morey, *"Outlines of Roman History," Forumromanum*, 2009, https://www.forumromanum.org/history/morey08.html.

7   Claire Breay, "Magna Carta: An introduction," *British Library Online*, July 2014, https://www.bl.uk/magna-carta/articles/magna-carta-an-introduction.

8   Ibid.

9   Lloyd Duhaime, "Solon's Laws: Greece," *Duhaime Legal Information*, October 2006, http://www.duhaime.org/LawMuseum/LawArticle-306/530 -BC--Solons-Laws-Greece.aspx.

10 Ryan Garrett, *Naked Statues, Fat Gladiators, and War Elephants: Frequently Asked Questions about the Ancient Greeks and Romans* (Prometheus Publishers: New York, 2021).

11 Lloyd Duhaime, "The-First-Law-School," *Duhaime Legal Information*, January 2013, http://www.duhaime.org/LawMuseum/LawArticle-1538/250 -The-First-Law-School.aspx.

12 Anton-Hermann Chroust, "Legal Profession during the Middle Ages: The Emergence of the English Lawyer Prior to 1400," *Notre Dame Law Review* vol. 31, no. 4, 1956, https://scholarship.law.nd.edu/cgi/viewcontent. cgi?article=3644&context=ndlr.

13 Ibid.

14 Ibid.

15 Ibid.

16 Gerald T. Bennett, "Let's Kill All the Lawyers! Shakespeare (Might Have) Meant It," *Florida Bar Journal*, vol. 72, no. 11 (December 1998), https://

www.floridabar.org/the/florida/bar/journal/lets-kill-all-the-lawyers
-shakespeare-might-have-meant-it/.

17 Ibid.

18 E.g., Murray S. Eckell, Esq., "Shakespeare's Tribute to Lawyers," *Delaware
County Daily Times* (August 19, 2002), https://www.eckellsparks.com
/newsletters/the-first-thing-we-do-lets-kill-all-the-lawyers/ (accessed
August 28, 2021).

19 Bennett, *Florida Bar Journal.*

20 Rachel Ellenberger, "Doubly Damned Attornies: Lessons on Professional
Regulation from Eighteenth-Century England," The *Georgetown Journal
of Legal Ethics* Vol. 32:577, https://www.law.georgetown.edu/legal-ethics
-journal/wp-content/uploads/sites/24/2019/11/GT-GJLE190028.pdf.

21 J. Baker, "Counsellors and Barristers. An Historical Study," The
Cambridge Law Journal, 27(2), 205-229. Retrieved July 18, 2021, from
http://www.jstor.org/stable/4505317.

22 Anton-Hermann Chroust, "Legal Profession in Colonial America," *Notre
Dame Law Review* vol. 33, no. 4, 1957, https://scholarship.law.nd.edu/cgi
/viewcontent.cgi?article=3545&context=ndlr (entire section).

23 Ibid.

24 Dorsey Bodeman, et al., Maryland State Archives, "Margaret Brent (1601-
1671)," *Exploring Maryland's Roots: Library*, https://mdroots.thinkport.org
/library/margaretbrent.asp (accessed August 29, 2021).

25 W. Hamilton Bryson, "The History of Legal Education in Virginia,"
University of Richmond Law Review, vol. 14:155 (1979), https://scholarship
.law.wm.edu/cgi/viewcontent.cgi?article=1007&context=history; Harvard
Law School, "A Brief Timeline of Our First Two Centuries," *History of
Harvard Law School*, https://his.harvard.edu/about/history/ (accessed
August 29, 2021).

26 American Bar Association, "ABA Timeline," https://www.americanbar
.org/about_the_aba/timeline/, (accessed August 29, 2021).

27 Ibid.

28 Ibid.

29 John Leubsdorf, "Toward a History of the American Rule on Attorney
Fee Recovery," Vol. 47: No. 1, https://scholarship.law.duke.edu/cgi
/viewcontent.cgi?Article=3748&context=lcp.

30 *"The 1958 Lawyer and his 1938 Dollar,"* American Bar Association, Special
Committee on Economics of Law Practice, West Publishing Company
(1958), https://dcbar.org/getmedia/5ff404e1-f7fd-437a-9b67-c93a4782db08
/ABA-The-1958-lawyer_and_his_1938dollar.

31 *Goldfarb v. Virginia State Bar*, 421 U.S. 773 (1975); see also Sean Braswell,
"The Virginia Couple That Gave Birth to the Billable Hour," (OZY,
September 29, 2015), https://www.ozy.com/true-and-stories/the-virginia
-couple-that-gave-birth-to-the-billable-hour/60997/.

32   Jerome T. Barrett with Joseph P. Barrett, *A History of Alternative Dispute Resolution: The Story of a Political, Cultural, and Social Movement,* (Jossey-Bass, A Wiley Imprint, with The Association for Conflict Resolution, 2004).

33   Ibid.

34   Federal Judicial Center, "The Administration of the Federal Courts," *Timelines of Federal Judicial History,* https://www.fjc.gov/history/timeline/8286 (accessed August 30, 2021).

35   Ibid.

36   Dennis Nolan and Roger Abrams, "American Labor Arbitration: The Early Years," *University of Florida Law Review,* vol. xxxv, no. 3, (Summer 1983), https://repository.library.northeastern.edu/files/neu:332662/fulltext .pdf.

37   Ibid.

38   Ibid.

39   *AT&T Mobility LLC v. Concepcion,* 563 U.S. 333, 351 (2011).

40   American Arbitration Association, "Supplementary Rules for Class Arbitrations," (2011), www.adr.org/active-rules (accessed August 30, 2021).

41   Barrett, *History of Alternative Dispute Resolution.*

CHAPTER FOUR

1   For an intriguing exposé and in-depth analysis of the damaging impacts of excessive due process in the American legal system, and thoughtful prescriptions to correct them, see Philip K Howard, *The Death of Common Sense: How Law Is Suffocating America* (Random House: New York, 1994), and *Life Without Lawyers: Restoring Responsibility in America* (Random House: New York, 2009).

2   R. James Maxeiner, "What America Can Learn From Germany's Justice System," *The Atlantic* (June 2012), https://en.wikipedia.org/wiki/Judiciary of Germany.

3   James Savory and Berkeley Square Mediation, "*Psychological Factors Affecting Dispute Settlement,*" (October 2010), http://www .berkeleysquaremediation.com/wp-content/uploads/psychology-of-dispute -settlement1.pdf.

4   Donna Shestowsky, "How Litigants Evaluate the Characteristics of Legal Procedures: A Multi-Court Empirical Study," *UC Davis Law Review,* vol. 49 (2016): 793, 832, https://lawreview.law.ucdavis.edu/issues/49/3 /Articles/49-3 Shestowsky.pdf.

5   Ibid.

6   Ibid.

7   Ibid.

8   Donna Shestowsky, "Inside the Mind of the Client: An Analysis of
    Litigants' Decision Criteria for Choosing Procedures," *Conflict Resolution
    Quarterly*, vol. 36 (2018): 69.

9   Today, only where a wrong is committed anonymously—like a hit-and-
    run driver—is there much opportunity to truly flee and avoid dispute
    altogether.

10 National Center for State Courts ("NCSC"), "The Landscape of Civil
    Litigation in State Courts," *Civil Justice Initiative* (November 2015).

11 Paula Hannaford-Agor and Nicole L. Waters, "Estimating the Cost of
    Civil Litigation," *NCSC Court Statistics Project, Caseload Highlights, vol. 20,
    no. 1* (January 2013), https://www.srln.org/node/582/estimating-cost-civil
    -litigation-ncsc-2013.

12 American Arbitration Association (AAA), "B2B Dispute Resolution
    Impact Report," *2015 Key Statistics* (2016), http://go.adr.org/rs/294-SFS-516
    /images/AAA186_2015_B2B_Case_Statistics.pdf.

13 NCSC, "Estimating the Cost of Civil Litigation;" Paula Hannaford-
    Agor, Robert C. LaFountain, and Shauna Strickland, "Trial Trends and
    Implications for the Civil Justice System," *NCSC Caseload Highlights:
    Examining the Work of the State Courts, vol. 11, no. 3* (June 2005).

14 NCSC, "The Landscape of Civil Litigation in State Courts;" AAA, "B2B
    Dispute Resolution Impact Report;" David Trubek et al. "The Costs of
    Ordinary Litigation," *Civil Litigation Research Project (CLRP), UCLA Law
    Review*, vol. 31, 72-127 (October 1983); Hannaford-Agor, "Estimating
    the Cost of Civil Litigation;" and Hannaford-Agor, "Trial Trends and
    Implications."

15 Ibid.

16 Herbert Kritzer, "The Civil Litigation Research Project: Lessons for
    Studying the Civil Justice System," *Proceedings of the Second Workshop
    on Law and Justice Statistics 1983* (U.S. Department of Justice, Bureau of
    Justice Statistics, 1984), https://www.ojp.gov/ncjrs/virtual-library/abstracts
    /civil-litigation-research-project-final-report-volume-1-studying; Trubek,
    "The Costs of Ordinary Litigation."

17 Ibid.

18 Roy Weinstein et al , "Efficiency and Economic Benefits of Dispute
    Resolution through Arbitration Compared with U.S. District Court
    Proceedings," *Micronomics Economic Research and Consulting* (March
    2017).

19 Kritzer, "Lessons for Studying the Civil Justice System."

20 Frank Strong, "What Size is the Addressable US Legal Market?"
    Corporate Counsel (January 15, 2015) (Small Law 2 Comments); Legal
    Executive Institute, "How Big is the US Legal Services Market?" (January
    11, 2016).

21 NCSC, "The Landscape of Civil Litigation in State Courts."

CHAPTER FIVE

1   *Henry VI*, part 2, Act 4, Scene 2. http://shakespeare.mit
    .edu/2henryvi/2henryvi.4.2.html. See the Shakespearean *SIDEBAR* and
    brief discussion in Chapter 3.
2   Wikipedia contributors, "Paul Harvey" and "The Rest of the Story,"
    Wikipedia, The Free Encyclopedia, https://en.wikipedia.org/wiki/Paul
    _Harvey and https://en.wikipedia.org/wiki/The_Rest_of_the_Story
    (accessed August 20, 2021).

CHAPTER SIX

1   Neuroscience today well recognizes the substantial harmful effects and
    costs of sustained stress and anxiety as noted in Christophe Morin, *"The
    Serenity Code: How Brain Plasticity Helps You Live Without Stress,
    Anxiety and Depression (SAD)"* (Depth Insights, 2020).

CHAPTER SEVEN

1   Nicole L. Waters, "Caseload Highlights: Court Statistics Project,"
    Examining the Work of the State Courts, vol.14, no.1 (National Center for
    State Courts, March 2007); Civil Trials on Appeal, https://www.ncsc
    .org_data/assets/pdf_file/0029/23969/vol14num1civiltrialsonappeal1.pdf.
2   National Opinion Research Center (NORC) at the University of Chicago,
    *The Justice Gap: Measuring the Unmet Civil Legal Needs of Low-Income
    Americans* (Legal Services Corporation (LSC), 2017). LSC is the single
    largest funder of civil legal aid for low-income Americans. Established in
    1974, LSC operates as an independent 501(c)(3) nonprofit corporation that
    promotes equal access to justice and provides grants for high-quality civil
    legal assistance to low-income Americans. LSC distributes more than
    90% of its total funding to 133 independent nonprofit legal aid programs
    in more than 800 offices. See https://www.lsc.gov/about.
3   Ibid.

CHAPTER EIGHT

1   Each case study in this chapter is based on my personal experience. For
    example, the NDR provider mentioned in the text was Just Resolve, the
    company I founded to administer NDR disputes.
2   *E.g., Annapolis Professional Firefighters Local 1926 v. City of Annapolis, 642
    A.2d 889, 893-895 (Md. Ct. Spec. App. 1994)* (In enforcing an agreement to
    use mediation and neutral fact-finding, the court held that "[A] written
    agreement to submit either an existing or a future dispute to a form of

alternative dispute resolution that is not otherwise against public policy will be enforced at least to the same extent that it would be enforced if the chosen method were arbitration"); *AMF, Inc. v. Brunswick Corp., 621 F. Supp. 456, 461 (EDNY 1985)* (a non-adversarial, but otherwise arbitration-like alternative dispute resolution method is enforceable).

3   Alternatively, one might see it as a vaccine that prevents or cures most cases of the targeted affliction.

CHAPTER NINE

1   See California Rules of Professional Conduct, Rule 1.1. See also the American Bar Association's Model Rules of Professional Conduct, Rule 1.1, adopted in numerous states, which reads similarly.

2   See the blog Seán Kenehan, "Not Invented Here Syndrome Explained," *Learnosity* (2006), https://learnosity.com/not-invented-here-syndrome -explained/, and other online search sources using this term.

3   See Carol Dweck, *Mindset—The New Psychology of Success* (New York: Random House, 2006); Adam Grant, *Think Again, The Power of Knowing What You Don't Know* (New York: Viking Press, 2021).

4   Ibid.

5   Wikipedia free encyclopedia; The Marketing Accountability Standards Board, common language marketing dictionary, www.themasb.org.

6   Claire Payton, "Uncola: Seven-Up, Counterculture and the Making of an American Brand," *Duke University Libraries* (Hartman Center, Duke University Department of History, December 4, 2017), https://blogs .library.duke.edu/rubenstein/2017/12/04/uncola/.

7   Wikipedia, The Free Encyclopedia, "Ombudsman," (accessed August 25, 2021), https://en.wikipedia.org/wiki/Ombudsman.

8   E.g., American Bar Association, "Neutral Fact Finding," (accessed August 25, 2021), https://www.americanbar.org/groups/dispute_resolution /resources/DisputeResolutionProcesses/neutralfact-finding/.

9   Wikipedia, The Free Encyclopedia, "Videotape format war," (accessed August 25, 2021), https://en.wikipedia.org/wiki/Videotape_format_war.

10   Sean Flaherty, "Trust: How to Use Technology to Generate Trust," (ITX Corporation, 2021) ("Flaherty, ITX Trust White Paper"), www.itx.com, https://itx.com/strategy/trust-how-to-use-technology-to-generate-trust/.

11   Stephen M. R. Covey, *The Speed of Trust, The One Thing That Changes Everything*, (CoveyLink, Simon & Schuster, Inc., 2006).

12   Flaherty, ITX Trust White Paper.

13   Ibid.

14   Americans have this reputation, and probably deservedly so by most comparative measures, though reliance on any one measure can mislead. See, J. Mark Ramseyer and Eric B. Rasmusen, "Comparative Litigation

Rates," Harvard Law School, John M. Olin Center for Law, Economics and Business, Discussion Paper No. 681 (November 2010), available at http://www.law.harvard.edu/programs/olin_center/ and at http://ssrn.com/.

15　Philip K. Howard, *Life Without Lawyers: Restoring Responsibility in America*, (New York: Random House, 2009), and Philip K. Howard, *The Death of Common Sense: How Law is Suffocating America*, (New York: Random House, 1994). Affected conduct ranges far and wide, encompassing absurd warning labels, cancelled community festivals, closed playgrounds, and teacher discipline of unruly students.

16　Larry P. Arnn, "Thoughts on the Current Crisis," Imprimis (Hillsdale College, March/April 2020), Vol. 49, No. 3/4, https://imprimis.hillsdale.edu/thoughts-current-crisis/.

CHAPTER TEN

1　W. Chan Kim and Renée Mauborgne, *Blue Ocean Strategy: How to Create Uncontested Market Space and Make the Competition Irrelevant*, (Boston: Harvard Business School Press, 2004).

CHAPTER ELEVEN

1　Paddy Chayefsky (writer), Sidney Lumet (director), Howard Gottfried and Fred C. Caruso (producers), *Network* [motion picture], (Metro-Goldwyn-Mayer, 1976.)

ABOUT THE AUTHOR

Robert Christopher is a recovering attorney, lawsuit reformer, and businessperson. An AV Preeminent rated litigation and trial attorney,* his legal career spans over 40 years and has included roles as lead trial counsel in both state and federal courts, regional managing partner at a top global law firm, general counsel of his family's farm business, mediator, arbitrator, and settlement judge pro tem in his community's local trial courts.

Over the last decade, Rob has developed and now champions a new approach to delivering real and cost-effective justice in common limited stakes legal disputes through the use of a neutral-driven non-adversarial resolution process (NDR). His published articles on the subject have appeared in numerous periodicals ranging from the Association of Corporate Counsel's *Docket* to the California Lawyers Association's *California Litigation*, and the Global Electronics Publication *U.S. Tech*, and he has founded an independent neutral service, Just Resolve, to evangelize adoption and use of the method. Learn more at www.justresolve.com.

Rob lives in Morgan Hill, California, with his wife of over 40 years. When not trying to disrupt wasteful lawsuits, he enjoys playing tennis, acting and singing in amateur community stage productions, volunteering and doing board service for his community's charitable foundation, and sharing time and love with his growing family that now boasts four grandchildren.

per leading attorney directory publisher Martindale-Hubbell

www.ingramcontent.com/pod-product-compliance
Lightning Source LLC
Chambersburg PA
CBHW011845200326
41597CB00028B/4708